POWER STRUCTURE AND URBAN POLICY:
Who Rules in Oakland?

POLICY IMPACT
AND POLITICAL CHANGE
IN AMERICA
KENNETH M. DOLBEARE, Consulting Editor

Designed as brief supplements for American Government and other undergraduate political science courses, books in this series confront crucial issues of public policy in the United States. The primary goal of the series is to demonstrate the utility of analytical concepts of political science for understanding the most pressing social and political problems of our time. Some books will be addressed to the question of how adequate present policies are to cope with current problems, and others will deal with questions of political change. Each book will be published in both soft- and cloth-cover editions.

HAYES: **POWER STRUCTURE AND URBAN POLICY: Who Rules in Oakland?**

RODGERS and BULLOCK: **LAW AND SOCIAL CHANGE: Civil Rights Laws and Their Consequences**

SHARKANSKY: **THE MALIGNED STATES: Policy Accomplishments, Problems, and Opportunities**

POWER STRUCTURE AND URBAN POLICY: Who Rules in Oakland?

EDWARD C. HAYES

Department of Political Science
University of Wisconsin

McGraw-Hill Book Company

New York   St. Louis   San Francisco   Düsseldorf   Johannesburg
Kuala Lumpur   London   Mexico   Montreal   New Delhi   Panama
Rio de Janeiro   Singapore   Sydney   Toronto

This book was set in Press Roman by Creative Book Services,
division of McGregor & Werner, Incorporated,
and printed and bound by The Murray Printing Company.
The designer was Barbara Ellwood.
The editor was Robert P. Rainier.
Ted Agrillo supervised production.

POWER STRUCTURE AND URBAN POLICY:
Who Rules in Oakland?

Library of Congress Catalog Card Number 79-37868

1234567890MUMU7987654321

FOR MY PARENTS

To be out of the moiling street
With its swelter and its sin!
Who has given me this sweet
And given my brother dust to eat?
And when will his wage come in?

William Vaughn Moody

CONTENTS

INTRODUCTION

Who rules, and for whom? Few questions can stir up as many important questions about politics as this one.[1] For it leads us immediately into a series of highly charged and important areas of analysis and conclusion. How, for example, should the researcher study political power? Do the methods he uses bias his findings?[2] To what extent does business have an over-all influence in urban politics, and are there single, or multiple pyramids of ruling power?[3] Are important decisions not made which should be made, due to the structure of the national or urban decision-making environment, and can certain social classes be identified as consistent winners or losers in the outcome of the policy process?[4]

Recent debates over these questions, while they have not created consensus among different writers and schools of thought, have clarified the issues involved in the study of community power and have made possible the development of the method used in this essay. While acknowledging my debt to the controversies of the past decade, in what follows I shall be using a tripartite methodology in an attempt to use, and go beyond, earlier methods. First, this essay will give empirical evidence on the process of power—who makes decisions and the structure of direct influence. In this regard the method of the essay is traditional. Secondly, it looks at the political system and infers the existence of power by judging from the consequences, or outputs, of the policy process and asks whose interests and priorities have been served by that process—in a word, who benefited? Finally, the essay bases itself on the significance of the urban economic system in creating problems and in limiting public policy solutions. Each of these aspects of method are interrelated. Let us look first at the question of benefits.

BENEFITS, PRIORITIES, AND INTERESTS

In its study of political power, political science has most often sought to trace direct influence from one private interest group or individual to public decisions.[5] Yet it is important to ask whether such a direct relationship is the only, or even the most important, way of analyzing political power. Even if there were no observable connections between private individuals and the decisions made by government, still those governmental decisions might well be biased in the interest of one sector of society and against the interest of another. Any such bias, or favored treatment of the priorities and interests of one sector of society that shows an enduring pattern over time, allows us to speak of the "benefits structure", the output side of a power structure.[6] If we find such a highly consistent pattern in the distribution of benefits, then we have located an extremely important relationship in the community, a constant that may be a better barometer of popular political moods and the functioning of the political system than the mathematical measurement of political power inputs. It is the question of whether such a consistent pattern of outputs exists, and in which areas, that will be examined in the following pages, including the areas of race, housing, urban redevelopment and model cities, public welfare, and poverty and job programs. In each of these areas we shall be asking who has benefited, and whose priorities have been followed. The discovery of such a pattern of benefits provides a strong basis for concluding that the direct connection between private interests and public policy makers *does* exist, if we will but look for it.

Since this study focuses on areas related to the basics of life for poor and working-class people, the interests which will be discussed are generally economic or socioeconomic. This does not deny that other varieties of interest exist—psychological or personal or political, strictly defined—but I have simply chosen this kind of interest as subject matter showing politics in clear and more easily measurable terms than less tangible interests.[7]

To analyze who benefits I will be looking at the city as a locus of social, political, and economic actors. James Madison, in *The Federalist Papers*, no. 10, divided the country into a landed interest, a mercantile interest, and a manufacturing interest and stated that the greatest source of conflict, or faction, was between those who had property and those who did not. In the last century, Karl Marx based his theory of history and economics on this same division. In this essay I shall be asking the extent to which certain major economic interests, primarily real estate and manufacturing, have come to influence public policy on issues of particular importance to them and the general character of the policy process as a whole. To do this I shall look first at the over-all character of political power and reform in the city over the past century, and then at specific areas of policy, asking of each a series of interrelated questions: who benefited from government policy? Whose priorities guided policy, and whose goals were realized? Did policy serve the broad interests of the poor and working-class communities directly affected by government activity, or did it primarily follow the interests of a governmental elite and particularly affected industries?

In following these questions we will be breaking new ground in the area of community power studies. Almost all previous studies have paid attention almost exclusively to the structure of influence—the input side of the governmental process—and only secondarily considered the question of the content of policy and who benefited from it. And, to sum up, a direct power connection, an identifiable chain of causal influence between private and public actors is a method which overlooks the crucial question of benefits.

POWER AND INFLUENCE: A LINK BETWEEN ECONOMIC STRATIFICATION AND PUBLIC POLICIES?

The second major aspect of the method of this study is to show the main outlines of the causal chain of policy influence, to do what previous studies of political influence have also done. In doing this we shall be treating government as a presumed independent variable, capable in theory of responding equally to pressures applied from any quarter. Given such a starting point we will be asking who, in fact, exercised either subtle or blatant political influence, and whether this chain of command ran from the propertied groups described by Madison and Marx, from labor or middle-class groups, or from neighborhood organizations—or from all three. Here we are simply concerned to trace the direct process of power, and to show who has been able to influence it the most on a long-term basis or at moments of heightened conflict.

In each area of policy making more or less constant conflict has arisen, not in every year in every area, but at certain defined points of the city's history. The General Strike which closed the city completely in 1946 is a notable instance of conflict, which generalized from a single issue to challenge the political authority of decision makers as a class. That there has not been constant conflict or frequent massive strikes does not mean that all sectors of Oakland's society are equally satisfied with or equally advantaged by the city's existing constitutional and policy-making arrangements; the years in which there were no slave revolts in the antebellum South far outnumber the years of revolt. Whenever conflict and protest has existed in Oakland's politics I have tried to show the relation of such protest to the policy process and to the question of who has benefited or been disadvantaged by that process.[8]

THE ECONOMY AND URBAN POLITICS

The third component of this essay's methodology relates the structure of the economic system, and the problems generated by it, to the performance of public policy makers. This is done by viewing the urban economy in two aspects: first, as a system of power in itself, highly organized and as much involved in the authoritative allocation of values as is the political system; second, as a major source of both economic and racial difficulties, problems which soon or late are brought to, or force their way into, the public arena for settlement. These problems include racial segregation in housing, discrimination in employment, and economic dependency.

The role of the economic system and its decision makers in contributing to social problems becomes one of considerable significance if, on inspection, government priorities turn out to be the same as or similar to corporate priorities, or if the government's programs fail to challenge corporate performance where necessary. If, for example, a housing shortage is endemic to the performance of the economy, than how can we defend a public housing policy which assumes the basic ability of private industry to supply an adequate amount of units for all income classes? Or, to take another example, if industry is so structured that it will never provide full employment, how meaningful is a public job or poverty program which assumes that industry will? Thus the question of whether the economic system has these built-in limitations is central to giving us a true perspective on the public policy process.

Together, these three elements—the functioning of the economy and its priorities; the linkage between private groups and their priorities, and governmental policy; and the distribution of policy benefits—are the main questions which define the methodology of this book

NOTES

1. This question was first raised about the urban scene in recent years by Floyd Hunter, *Community Power Structure*, Chapel Hill: University of North Carolina, 1953.
2. A wide variety of views on methods of studying community power and various findings can be found in Michael Aiken and Paul Mott, eds., *The Structure of Community Power*, New York: Random House, 1970; William Hawley and Fred Wirt, *The Search for Community Power*, Englewood Cliffs, N.J.: Prentice-Hall, 1969; and Terry N. Clark, ed., *Community Structure and Decision Making,* San Francisco: Chandler, 1968. See also M. Mankoff, "Power in Advanced Capitalist Societies: A Review Essay," *Social Problems,* Winter 1970.
3. See Clark, op. cit., chaps. 1-3; Robert Dahl, "Critique of the Ruling Elite Model," *American Political Science Review,* Jume 1958.
4. See Peter Bachrach and Morton Baratz, "Two Faces of Power," *American Political Science Review*, December 1962; and by the same authors, *Power and Poverty, Theory and Practice*, New York: Oxford University, 1970.
5. For a theoretical defense of this method see Robert Dahl, "The Concept of Power," *Behavioral Science*, July 1957.
6. A benefits structure is about what Gerhard Lenski means by "political privilege". See Lenski, *Power and Privilege; A Theory of Social Stratification*, New York: McGraw-Hill, 1966.

7. Using David Easton's language, this is the method of studying "the decisive allocation of values", defining values as economic benefits. See David Easton, *The Political System*, New York, Knopf, 1953; and Harold Lasswell, *Politics: Who Gets What, When, How*, New York: P. Smith, 1950.
8. For an analysis of protest in American cities see Michael Lipsky, *Protest in City Politics*, Chicago: Rand McNally, 1970; and S. P. Sethi, *Business Corporations and the Black Man—An Analysis of Social Conflict: The Kodak-FIGHT Controversy*, San Francisco: Chandler, 1970.

ACKNOWLEDGMENTS

This book could not have been written without the important help of many people. Professor Michael Rogin provided indispensable assistance throughout the preparation of the research and first writing. To Clyde Johnson, who provided insight and support, and Floyd Hunter, Mark Comfort, and Elijah Turner, who contributed in unique ways, acknowledgment is gladly given. Dozens of public and private citizens, more than can possibly be named separately, gave freely of their time and information. William F. Knowland generously allowed access to himself and his staff. The book could not have been done without the assistance of my editor, Ken Dolbeare, or Pam MacGregor, who kept me on course during the writing of the final draft.

EDWARD C. HAYES

POWER
STRUCTURE
AND URBAN
POLICY:
Who Rules
in Oakland?

PART

1

The Context of Urban Power

CHAPTER ONE

The Evolving
Corporate Structure

To analyze the extent to which business has influenced the politics of the city, we can begin with a distinction between direct influence, on the one hand, and the various conditions which create a context for direct influence. The direct involvement of the city's businessmen in the political process is a major subject of this book, including involvement in specific policy areas for specific goals and—in this and the following chapter—involvement of a leading newspaper in the general direction of the electoral and policy process as a whole.

But to understand such direct influence it is helpful to begin by looking at those underlying conditions which have provided the impetus to the growth and permanence of business political power, the conditions which facilitate the general political impact of the business sector. There are many factors which could be named, including specific laws which sanction large personal fortunes and the ownership of the mass media by big business itself.[1] But here we will examine only what seem to be two of the most important of these conditions: first, the prevailing American political-economic ideology; and second, the rise of, and private control over the large urban corporation, the structural revolution in the urban economy.

While economic structure and ideology may seem an unusual place to begin a study of political power and policy making, they nevertheless show something very important about urban business' political power: its sources. Ideology and economic structure, together with the ownership of corporations by private individuals, constitute the basic sources of political power of business and financial executives. The political philosopher James Harrington wrote in the seventeenth century that "Land is power"; so, to a large extent, are urban corporations the source of power for the owners and managers of corporations today. By looking first at the structure and ideology of these corporations and the economic system which they comprise, the following section should facilitate an understanding of both the extent and limits of business influence over specific policy areas discussed in the remaining chapters of this book.

Oakland, like any American city, has a market-directed economy. Almost without exception the city's economic institutions—its real estate industry, factories, stores, and banks—are privately owned. Goods, resources, and services are allocated through the mechanism of prices on the open market. The economy is not planned by government agencies, and private bondholders and shareholders realize a return on their investment in businesses whose purpose is to make as high as possible a net return, or profit. In short, Oakland is an example of urban American capitalism. Supporting this type of economic system is a national ideology, a system of values which emphasizes the private control of large industry, competition among enterprises and individuals, and acceptance of the existing distribution of wealth as largely justified by competition and the superior abilities and skills of the more wealthy social strata. This ideology, in America as in other countries and economic systems, both interprets and supports existing economic institutions.

Why should the type and ideology of the American economic system be of concern to this study? If we look carefully we can see an enormous political importance. Primarily, the values of the economic system, because they are assumed by the mass media and widely accepted by the mass public,[2] set the rules of the game for political activity in the city. First, these values (or this ideology) justify private direction of urban corporate wealth, thereby aiding private owners and managers to maintain their position in the economy that carries with it a high potential for access to political decisions. Secondly, by viewing poverty as unavoidable or based on individual laziness, these values create a general atmosphere of apathy towards poverty itself. This attitude, shared by almost all sectors of American society, blames the poor for their own poverty, not the economic environment in which the poor must function, and thereby creates a bias against which the poor must always contend, a stigma with which more affluent political actors need not contend.[3] Finally, the ideology of the economic system is quite closely related to the political ideology of liberalism—of limited powers, or the laissez-faire theory of the state. The private economy has traditionally preferred a limited-power state, so that its own freedom to set private economic policy, or to manipulate public policy, is maximized.[4] We shall see how Oakland's businessmen demanded this greater freedom against a strong commission form of government later in this chapter. But, taken together, the ideology of present American economy, including the belief in competition, private corporate control, and the acceptance of large income inequalities, creates a social context in which the political influence of the corporation is maximized, and hence constitutes a basic factor underlying business' direct influence.

A second underlying source of direct political influence of urban business has been the rise of the privately owned, giant urban corporation. This economic change has created a new set of political demands, new inputs into the urban political system. The transformation of Oakland—from a squatters' town of rough wooden shacks, dominated by a few ambitious businessmen who succeeded first in incorporating the town and then in ceding its valuable waterfront to one of their business associates[5] —to a modern metropolis with a population of some 365,000, based on heavy industry and a highly developed system of roads and harbors, has created new rules of the game for the city's political policy-making process. Policies adequate for assisting the commercial elite in the nineteenth century are totally inadequate for managing a developed industrial society of the 1970s. Hence the transformation of the city's economic type and structure, from commercial to industrial, has created a new set of political-economic demands—for freeways, supply of workers, adequate housing, and general social stability—which the city is called on to provide or insure. Business is partly able to enforce these requirements on urban government by a variety of techniques, of which the most powerful is the simple threat to leave town; or, if the crime and poverty of a city is too high for any simple government remedies, and if the corporations have too large an investment in the city to easily relocate, business can enter into broad programs to renew the downtown areas—a pattern of involvement which exists in almost every important city today. This does not mean that business-sponsored renewal will be a success even for businessmen, or take place without substantial costs in human and economic terms, but it does mean that we should expect business involvement in city affairs whenever the operating requirements of the urban corporation require it. Those requirements may even outrun the abilities of the city charter to provide needed corporate economic infrastructure—roads, sewage systems, low enough taxes, or other preferred policies. When this point is reached we might expect business pressures for revision of the charter, a phenomenon we will be examining later in this chapter.

To understand the significance of the city's present economic structure we must look at the evolution and major components of that structure. In 1925, 602 establishments in the city created a gross product of some $144,840,830, of which the amount added by manufacturers was around $58,000,000.[6] By 1939, value added by manufacturers had risen to $68,282,933, produced by 599 establishments; in 1954 value added had risen to $377,061,000,[7] and total establishments numbered 824; and by 1967, the last available figures, value added had grown to $417,100,000, and the total establishments had dropped to 748. Total establishments employing over 20 persons dropped from 264 in 1954 to 243 in 1967, while value added in the same period rose by around $35 million—indicating some tendency toward concentration of productive assets.

The Depression accounts for the relatively slow growth of value added between 1925 and 1939; World War II accounts for the mushrooming growth between 1939 and 1954, and for the growth in Oakland and the Bay Area generally of certain war-baby corporations that thrived on military contracts.

Overall, this 50-year growth period, stimulated by two world wars, has led to the expansion of large manufacturing and transportation-related corporations, including: Kaiser Industries; Owens-Illinois Glass Company; Montgomery Ward and Company; Transamerica Corporation; Sunshine Biscuit Company; Standard Oil Company of California; Shell Oil Company; Bank of America; Sears, Roebuck and Company; Mack Truck; Dodge Truck Division of Chrysler Motors; Mead Paper Company; the Southern Pacific, Western Pacific, and Santa Fe Railroads; Pacific Telephone and Telegraph Company; the Pacific Gas and

Electric Company; and the Oakland *Tribune*. All of the above have headquarters or major branches in Oakland. Many of them are active in local and regional politics, especially in areas of urban renewal (see Chapter Five), county taxation levels (see this chapter and Chapter Four), the city port authority, and the Bay Area Council (see Chapter Eight). Two of these corporations, Kaiser Industries and the *Tribune*, have been involved in the city's politics in so many ways and for such a long period that we can call them political activist corporations (for a further definition of this concept, see Chapter Seven). They, like the other big urban corporations, owe their corporate existence, their large size, and their resulting economic power base, to the trend towards growth and gigantism in the city and national economies. Kaiser employs over 10,000 persons and the *Tribune* over 5,000, placing them among the top 25 employers in the city, with as many employees as Oakland had citizens in the 1870s. Safeway stores has had a vice-president on the Oakland School Board throughout the 1960s, the president of Howard Terminals (Oakland), one of the largest ship terminal corporations in the world, was the spearhead of the city's 1958 school bond issue campaign; and the Bank of America has often had an official sitting as a director of the county park commission. We shall examine later in this chapter and throughout the book the total amount of influence, the ways it is exercised, and the relation of the political system to demand inputs of corporate and commercial business. Here we simply make note of the growth of the corporation and the political potential afforded the corporation which chooses to enter politics.

The housing industry likewise has shown a transformation in structure. In this industry there is abundant evidence of concentration in production. Before World War II, the majority of houses in Oakland were built by individual house builders; tract housing was almost non-existent. But the World War transformed the structure of the industry; by 1949 large builders in the Bay Area, those builders who constructed over 100 houses per year, built 35 percent of all the housing in that year—although they were only 2 percent of the total number of builders.[8] By 1960, large housebuilders accounted for 74 percent of all housing units built in the northern California area.[9] The banking industry, on which the real estate industry largely depends, had also become heavily concentrated by the 1960s. The Depression and war ended much of the independence of Oakland banks; today, much if not the majority of the city's banking wealth is owned by nonlocal banks such as First California Western and the Bank of America. By 1950 there were only about a dozen sources of money supply for tract construction loans in the Bay Area; six banks actually accounted for about 90 percent of the loans, and the two largest banks furnished more than half the total,[10] a very high rate of concentration.

As a consequence of the trend toward banking concentration, the number of banks on which local city realtors depend is likewise limited. Again, this economic structure has a profound impact on society and politics. The social policies of a very few commercial banks on issues with an enormous public impact, such as loans for integrated housing or the availability of money for low-income housing construction, became in fact the prevailing policies for the city as a whole. And local realtors can, in a more concentrated industry, more easily act as private legislators of public housing and safety codes. The involvement of city realtors in discriminatory housing practices, and the city's willingness to tolerate these practices, are outlined in Chapter Four; the city real estate board's activities in writing the city's fire, ventillating, and related housing codes is discussed in Chapters Four and Five. The exact extent of the political power of the real estate industry is dealt with in those chapters in some detail. Here we wish to point out that it is the fact of private control over the real estate industry by a relatively small number of firms, and the increasing concentration of the house building and financial firms, that blurs the distinction between public and private policies, while creating the context for successful industrial intervention in the political process.

We can now ask again: how important are the ideology, structure, and fact of private ownership of the urban economy to the political influence of urban corporate owners and managers? To answer this question we might imagine, for example, that the poor of any city had major control over that city's dozen largest banks and corporations. What would such a situation mean for the city's politics? First, with such wealth at their command, loans to the poor could become easier, hence reducing if not eliminating one potent source of political conflict. The leading executives of the poor-directed banks could make large contributions to a poor people's party, and perhaps win control of city hall by the electoral process. And the banks together might sponsor low- or no-profit corporations to build schools housing, and recreation facilities in declining or slum areas. Finally, the corporations together could provide free time for both executives and workers to engage in massive voter registration drives among the poor and nonwhite neighborhoods. Obviously, such activities would mean that control over government and public policies would shift substantially in favor of the poor, compared to the present situation in American cities. The obvious difference between the above example and the real situation of American cities lies in the fact that the present owners and managers of the large urban corporations do not choose to engage in those programs just mentioned; hence, ownership and management of the urban corporation can be seen as having a dramatic effect on the balance of *political* power in the city.

In opposition to the above view, many writers have argued recently that business plays only a marginal role in directly influencing urban policies.[11] From what has just been said, such an argument can be seen as partially valid. Most urban political leaders share the same values as urban businessmen, a fact which often makes direct business intervention in the political process less than urgent. And, indeed, there are obvious reasons for a corporation wanting either to stay out of politics, or at least to keep its name out of politics.

Yet, we must ask whether the failure of many, or even most, corporations to enter into highly *visible* political activities is the most important, or conclusive, empirical evidence on the subject of direct business power. We might ask, in questioning this evidence, why we should even expect business political activity—such as financing candidates—to be visible to the usual academic researcher; why large numbers of businesses should be involved in politics generally, when only certain issues, such as taxes and redevelopment, are of salient interest to the local corporation; and why many businesses should be involved, if *one* active corporation, or a business organization such as the chamber of commerce, is being heard at city hall? Massive business involvement in politics is quite unnecessary if any of the above conditions holds true.

Hence the view that business shuns politics, that there is a sharp bifurcation, or separation, of the business world from the political world, does not seem plausible. Given the existence of several dozen giant corporations, in Oakland as in many cities, corporations which are dependent on city services, low taxes, and "law and order" for smooth functioning, we might ask the following question: Is it possible to run such an urban industrial system *without* direct corporate demands on urban government? Is it possible to produce in Oakland half a billion dollars worth of goods, under a government which feels itself quite free of corporate imperatives? Much more likely is the proposition that *the economic system and the political process will be constantly interlaced, at as many points as the economic system has need or desire for political action, from franchises to police protection.* As a corollary to this proposition is the further proposition that urban businessmen, viewed as individuals whose personal incomes have grown enormously with the rise of the corporate form of economic organization, are very likely to act as financial sponsors for city and county projects that as individuals they may prefer for personal, as well as corporate, reasons. Such propositions would seem to be plausible starting points in an analysis of corporate political power.

We will begin our investigation of direct business political activity by looking at business efforts to change the city's charter system, the basic constitutional arrangements which govern the city. The ideological and structural context of business infiltration into the policy process has been outlined above. In the following pages we will start our search for direct business influence with the key question of the structure of urban government itself, not only to show the degree of business influence, but the consequences of business-inspired reforms and the revolt against city policies by the labor movement in 1946. This first examination of business activity should tell us something about the over-all power of business in the city, and something about who has benefited from the city's reformed institutions. And it will show us how a large corporation that *is* active in politics, Oakland's major newspaper and its publishers, can engage in politics in a most effective way.

BUSINESS INFLUENCE: CHARTER REFORM

At the turn of the present century the city's commercial and corporate businessmen exerted a highly visible political influence. In some areas, such as land use, the real estate industry was itself the decisive decision maker; in the absence of any city planning department until 1911 there was really no city agency to rival the power of the private sector over land planning. The city's businessmen were engaged in other areas of city policy making with varying degrees of success. For over a decade the Southern Pacific railroad won almost exclusive control over the city's valuable waterfront property, control which excluded small businessmen, whose candidate, George C. Pardee (see Table 2-7), succeeded in winning the office of mayor and limiting the railroad's influence.[12] The utilities engaged in a constant battle for political influence and cheap franchises; built railroad tracks down the center of important streets; pushed the city to pay large shares of the cost of railroad overpasses; and for purposes of increasing their own economic gain, intruded themselves into the political process with observable success. The fact of economic power in politics was never far out of sight.

But the process of corporate growth, the development of large manufacturing capabilities and attendant growth of an urban industrial work force, led to consequences which *forced* business to face the question of charter reform. This question was imposed by two problems: the need to lower taxes and encourage greater industrial development; and the need, or wish, to destroy the power of the revolutionary Socialist party, whose working class following mushroomed in Oakland as it did nationally.[13] In the 1911 city elections, the Socialists—in the name of working class revolution and nationalization of the corporations—polled 9,837 votes; the winning property party polled 11,732. Faced with this labor opposition the city's business and professional groups convened a meeting of freeholders, comprised almost entirely of business and social peers, and including the top officials of local banks, to draw up a new city charter, giving Oakland the commission form of government. Under this form, instead of a separate city council and separate directors for fire, public works, and other city departments, city commissioners combined the roles of councilmen (legislators) and department directors (executives).

The result of this meeting was a campaign in which the role of the city's businessmen was stated by the Chamber of Commerce's letter:

> The Oakland Chamber of Commerce had been very active in the campaign for the new type of city government, and to the Chamber belongs credit for a municipal fund to be used in advertising and entertaining.[14]

The economic benefits which accrued to business when the commission charter was passed have been described as follows:

> Much of the money saved by commission and manager governments was used to promote and aid local business interests. The Commission in Oakland, California for example, floated a bond issue of $2.5 million for harbor improvements and at the same time imposed a tax of two and half cents per $100 for municipal advertising and entertainment of visitors.[15]

The political benefits were also substantial. As happened in other cities, the new charter forbade the use of party labels on the ballot, requiring the so-called nonpartisan ballot, and, as had happened in other cities at about the same time, the result was to decimate the Socialist party vote in 1913.[16] Thus local business proved itself quite capable of directly intervening in the process of politics to create a charter of major value to itself.

At the same time, the political system created by the reform of 1911 had consequences which local entrepreneurs had not foreseen. The highly concentrated power of city government, with both executive and legislative power resting exclusively in the hands of five commissioners, gave the government a certain autonomy from private economic interests, and an ability to play one business faction off against another. So did the political following of the city's long-time Mayor, John Davie, a self-styled populist and small businessman who for a time ran a passenger ferry in competition with the Southern Pacific. Thus while the Socialists were eliminated and city policy on taxes was brought into line with business desires, the election of mayors and councilmen remained partially outside the control of local big business, and out of control of the Oakland *Tribune* and its publisher Joseph Knowland. Throughout the 1920s the *Tribune* referred to Davie and his county level counterpart, Mike Kelly, the sometimes liberal Republican politician who controlled the vote on the county board of supervisors, as bosses. This control by the politicians meant that policy could not be directed from the *Tribune;* and, as a corollary, it meant that whoever had a majority on the city council could appoint the city's port commissioner, a post which carried with it both control of policy and patronage. As a result, the port remained outside the easy control of the city's shipping interests and led the shipping companies, with the newspaper, to support governmental reform for a second time in this century.

The second reform was clearly led by the city's banking and business fraternity. In 1928 a local banker organized the Council-Manager League to bring the city manager system to the city. Public outrage against the city's government was at a peak because of a scandal in paving contracts between the city and a local contractor; district attorney Earl Warren, who later became Chief Justice of the United States Supreme Court, put some of the city's most respectable citizens on the stand to testify.[17] The league also cried out against corruption; but it had a more important, and very practical, motive for reform. A local banker, supporting the manager system in a speech to the Oakland Kiwanis, remarked that the city's high tax rate was scaring away new industry; then, making reference to a three-year study made by the Oakland Council-Manager League of other cities which adopted the manager system, he stated:

> We found that in every community of comparable size to ours, the tax rate decreased after the adoption of the city manager form of government. (The tax rate in Cincinnati) is constantly being de- creased under the city manager form of government.[18]

After this speech Kiwanis voted to endorse the council-manager plan; so did the city's Lion's club; so, too, did the *Tribune,* which editorialized in favor of the plan on numerous occasions and which printed most of the events and speeches of proponents of the plan and virtually nothing about the opposition.[19] The (Hearst) *Post-Inquirer* was equally one-sided. As a result, in the election of 1931 the council- manager amendments to the old charter passed easily, and practically all of the old commissioners, including Mayor Davie, were defeated.

The result was a charter system which augmented the power of business over city policy generally and of the *Tribune* over political elections. The first city manager ordered a pay slash for city employees and used the savings to lower city tax rates on business and residential property; the next manager, who held the job from 1933 to 1954 almost uninterruptedly (see pp. 35-36) was himself a vice-president of a leading Oakland bank. The charter created a semi-autonomous port commission whose directors to the present day have been largely businessmen, its revenues used almost entirely to improve the harbor facilities for corporate shippers. The defeat of Davie and the creation of the citywide method for elections abolished strong ward candidates and gave the newspapers' endorsements and selective news coverage a greater role in local elections. Thus both the interests of the city's business establishment, and the *Tribune's* political clout, were advanced at a stroke.

CONSOLIDATION OF A NEWSPAPER-CENTERED COALITION

The Knowland family was of major significance to the politics of the city. J. R. Knowland, editor, publisher, and owner of the Oakland *Tribune,* founded the political dynasty which has been to Oakland what the famous X family was to Middletown, or the Uihleins, owners of the Schlitz brewery, have been to the city of Milwaukee. The influence of the Knowland family has run through every facet of city life, from civic functions to social life to political influence. To understand this dynasty, and the political significance of its present representative, we must look at the man who built it.

In the early decades of this century J. R. Knowland was a member of the board of directors of several leading Oakland area banks. By the end of his life Knowland had been Advisory Director and member of the Executive Committee of the Wells Fargo Bank, and Director of Smith-Corona-Marchant, Inc., the California-Pacific Title Insurance Company, the California State Automobile Association, and the Associated Press. He had also served on numerous civic and philanthropic organizations, in the United States Congress and state Senate, and was a member, with Herbert Hoover and the social-corporate elite of the nation, of the Bohemian Club.[20] This array of directorates and club memberships gave Knowland, already known as a stand-pat Republican, access to the ideas and political support of the state and national corporate officials.

Through ownership of the newspaper, which he acquired in 1938 by means sharply criticized at the time,[21] Knowland added substantially to his base of influence. As bank and corporate director he already had an income far above average; now, as owner and publisher of the *Tribune,* he had undisputed control of one of California's four leading Republican newspapers,[22] one that, due to its mass circulation on the east side of San Francisco Bay, was already a major political force.

During the 1930s Knowland became a leading power in state and national Republican circles, serving on both state and county central committees and attending numerous national conventions as delegate. This influence was of benefit to his son William, the present publisher of the paper, in winning the Republican party nomination for United States senator in 1946. William F. Knowland subsequently won reelection to the Senate in 1952 and became, as majority and then minority leader, possibly the second most influential Republican in country, after the President, Dwight D. Eisenhower.

At the county board of supervisors, the elder Knowland, without ever holding an elective office, made himself the county's leading political figure. Mike Kelly, the political boss who controlled the board until the mid-1920s, was totally defeated by Earl Warren in 1925 when Warren persuaded a majority of the board of supervisors to appoint him, over Mike Kelly's nominee, as county district attorney. Knowland then supported Warren throughout the latter's political career, with the brief exception of the paving company scandals, and gave full newspaper support to all of Warren's numerous elections. The *Tribune* has also, by virtue of its position as the city's only big newspaper, been able to prevent the election of any Democrat or liberal to the office of district attorney down to the present day, while the board of supervisors, largely because of the newspaper's public positions, remains conservative and largely Republican.

Few people in the county's politics were neutral toward J. R. Knowland or ignorant of his power. Friend and foe alike recognized his considerable political influence, which was variously described to this writer as "great," "the leading political force in the county," "a rival with Mike Kelly," and "a father confessor to the board (of supervisors)." And the results of the Republican control, led by the newspaper, can be clearly seen in recent years. Of 19 directors of county departments, offices, and agencies in 1966, 13 were Republican, almost 70 percent of the total; 5 were Democratic; and 1 was independent. This was after eight years of Democratic control of a governor's office which has the power to fill vacancies on county boards of supervisors. In contrast, in the year 1960 only 45.6 percent of county voters were registered Republicans and 54 percent were registered Democrats, figures which testify to the continuing local power of a political machine whose foundations were laid over 30 years ago.

Knowland also enjoyed an unparalled *direct* influence over the city's politics. After the defeat of Davie and the creation of the council-manager form of government, the conservative business viewpoint was predominant in city policies. Within this framework one person, city auditor Harry Williams, became a source of independent political influence. The power of Mr. Williams, himself the operator of a small coal business, is described by his successor who served under him in the same office:

> Williams was a good friend of Mike Kelly, and probably of John Hassler at the Central Bank. Williams had to sign all the warrants for city expenditures. When he found a person or item he didn't quite like, or if somebody whispered in his ear, he would scotch someone's expenditure. Williams couldn't decide elections, but he acted as a kind of third government in city hall.[23]

But in 1941 Williams died, and Mike Kelly, already a defeated figure in county politics, passed away in the same year, with results described by a close observer:

> When both Kelly and Williams left the Oakland scene, they left no lieutenants to take their place. So the city politicians turned to the *Tribune.* The *Tribune* had not taken a hand in local politics as much as state and federal politics, as when it backed Earl Warren, a *Tribune* man, for governor. But when Williams died, Knowland was turned to, and he did take charge of the city.[24]

Thus there existed in the city after 1941 a period in which a newspaper publisher became the director of the city's political affairs, a situation which suggests that, in Oakland, the mid-twentieth century found one private corporation more involved in city politics than ever before.

We should note that, in its rise to power, the newspaper depended on political factors not immediately under its control. The strong role of the Republican party before the 1930s was an enormous help. The generally weak role played by labor in Oakland politics, as in much of the California political scene, aided the ideology and ascendency of business politics, helping the Republican party to long terms in office. One Oakland realtor and his son, the Breed family, held the county's state senate seat for some forty years; Breed, Knowland, and Warren were all Masons, members of the same lodge. Both the *Tribune* and its leading rival, the (Hearst) *Post-Inquirer,* were Republican. (The *Post-Inquirer* went out of business, suddenly, in 1953.) Thus the consolidation of the paper's political control was not simply due to the political skills and economic connections of its publishers, but to historical circumstances which have not remained entirely unchanged.

THE REVOLT OF LABOR: BUSINESS AND THE CHARTER UNDER ATTACK

What is striking in the history of these charter reforms is the ability of the Council-Manager League to secure passage of the new charter in the face of labor opposition. Labor's priorities—more and easier relief, the free right to organize and strike, and demands for greater public services—were all denied by both city and county government during this period. While the CIO was organizing Alameda County during the 1930s, Attorney General Earl Warren received a consignment of five Thompson submachine guns from the chief inspector of police of New York City.[25] The mayor of the city spoke to a large rally in 1938 to "expose" the CIO as anti-labor and Communist-controlled. On at least one occasion the Oakland police were found by the National Labor Relations Board to be actively assisting in strikebreaking,[26] while accusations of brutality against the police by labor organizers were common (See Chapter Two, note 16).

The city's businessmen were used to dealing with labor and to coopting certain of its leaders to maintain labor harmony in the city. In the period 1930-1950, six AFL union officials served in city government, two of them as mayor. None ever publicly defended the organizing activities of local labor, all had a craft union outlook, and two were registered Republicans.

One, Charles Real, head of the teamsters' local, declared his political position to be close to that of the city's employers. Real, a Republican, headed the county campaign committee for Earl Warren and presidential aspirant Thomas E. Dewey in 1948 and endorsed William F. Knowland of the *Tribune* for United States Senate in 1946.[27] Another labor leader, who served on the city council from 1933 to 1942, was both editor of the county labor press and president of the Building Trades

Council, and through the pages of his newspaper regularly endorsed the same Republican candidates for local office as did the *Tribune*. Three of the six unionists were small businessmen; two were registered Republicans; five of the six sat on the city council, and all of these received unqualified endorsement of the *Tribune* for their stints in office. All either endorsed or went along with the council majority during these decades, a majority whose main policies included fiscal stringency, hostility to CIO labor organizing, and support for the existing charter. As a result, any relief for the poor or working classes during the Depression was not forthcoming from this council; indeed, the one attempt by New Deal Democrats to win control of the council was easily brushed aside by the paper and council incumbents in 1937, and up to the late 1960s the Republican party maintained a clear majority on the council. Thus the city's business-political establishment coopted certain labor leaders to insure support for business priorities on major policy positions.

The attitudes of the rank-and-file worker toward this kind of labor leadership worsened as the Depression deepened. Discontent with conditions in the factory is suggested by the rapid organization of workers by the CIO, which grew by over 2,500 members in the years 1936-1940. This was a gradual process, but in 1946, labor's political involvement became explosive, expressed through the most powerful weapon that urban unions have—the general strike.

The General Strike of all Oakland city locals in 1946 led to a radicalization of labor attitudes; a mass mobilization of its energies to win control of the city government through the ballot box; and the projection of a program for reform in line with working-class interests. The contrast between what the city's business-oriented government had offered, and the program demanded by the mobilized blue-collar workers indicate the extent of labor dissatisfaction with the city government's historic policies. As a challenge to the power system built up by city business over the preceding decades, the labor revolt of the postwar years came closer to dethroning the local paper than any insurgent force since.[28] We can understand the durability of the prevailing coalition best by observing that revolt as it progressed, and how it was defeated.

LABOR STRIKES BACK: "TAKE THE POWER
OUT OF THE TOWER"

At 5:00 A.M. on Tuesday, December 3, 1946, twelve years after the San Francisco General Strike, the AFL trade unions of Alameda County called a general strike in Oakland.[29] The strike involved 142 unions, and an estimated 100,000 union members, and lasted for two days. It was the biggest strike which Oakland has seen before or since, and the chain of events leading up to it tells much about the political forces at work in the city.

In 1946 the Eastbay Retail Clerks attempted to organize Kahn's Department Store, and other downtown retail stores. According to one commentator, a meeting was held with District Attorney Ralph Hoyt, Oakland Police Chief Tracy, Sheriff H.P. Gleason, and leading business-men in November, 1946. The general theme of this meeting was reported to be: "Is the police department going to protect the property of the retail merchants?" Visible evidence of police sentiments was not long in coming.

At 2:00 A.M. Sunday, December 1, the police arrived at Kahn's and cleared the street of pickets, cut brake cables and towed away cars parked to block the delivery of supplies to the struck stores, and formed cordons, blocking access to the street. At 7:30 A.M. the police, in 12 radio cars and 15 motorcycles, escorted the first scab truck deliveries "with a show that has not been accorded even the President of the United States," according to local news commentary. The AFL labor leaders heading the clerk's strike called now for a general strike in retaliation.

All the city councilmen who spoke on the subject publicly came out against the General Strike. Mayor Herbert Beach, President and General Manager of the Beach-Krahn Amusement Company, declared that "The so-called 'general strike' is not a labor dispute. It is an attempt to push aside the government created by all the people." On Thursday, City Manager John Hassler, who earlier had agreed with labor's demands to allow the strike to continue at Kahn's now publicly stated: "I expect the stores to open and I expect to give protection to the stores." Labor, which had called off the General Strike after Hassler had promised to remain neutral, accused the City Manager of a double cross. But the threat to call another general strike was never carried out. On Friday, a group of 1,200 employers and businessmen met in the Oakland Auditorium to give Hassler, recently an official of the Central Bank of Oakland, "a unanimous vote of confidence."

Ultimately the Kahn's strike was settled. But during the course of the struggle the main elements of power in the city's government—mayor, city manager, city council, and police—had acted or spoken on behalf of the employers, sometimes in a decisive manner. So had city official Charles Real of the teamsters, who on February 1, 1947, pulled out of the Kahn's strike and out of the Central Labor Council, actions which brought his condemnation by the Building Trades Council as "unfit for office in state labor."

The General Strike laid the groundwork for the city's most important political revolt at the polls in this century. For the first time all branches of the trade union movement in the city and county—the railroad brotherhoods, the AFL-CIO unions, and the construction trades—were united in oppostion to the city government's conduct, and put up a slate of five candidates for city council. Winning five seats on a city council of nine would have given labor control of the council for the first time in history. The campaign which followed took on, as a result, the characteristics of a life and death struggle against the *Tribune*-centered political coalition.

In previous elections the newspaper had simply endorsed its favorite candidates for council and urged voters, on the day of election, to get out to the polls. In 1947 this format was changed. For the first and last time since at least 1931, the paper fully publicized the fact that voters in each of Oakland's seven councilmanic districts were legally entitled to vote for council candidates in all seven districts—a fact not generally known among Oakland voters. In addition, the paper spent many column inches, weeks in advance of the election, giving favorable publicity to the record of the incumbents, and pointing out the political liabilities of the five challengers.

Redbaiting, a technique which the national press has employed periodically, was used constantly by the *Tribune* during the 1947 campaign as a major political tactic. On May 12, 1947, the day before the general (runoff) election, the *Tribune* came out with an editorial which stated:

Briefly, these are the facts. The Communist Party of the United States announced a program of concentrating on school boards and city council campaigns. Oakland has been selected as one of the cities. At a May Day Communistic mass meeting recently held in Oakland, one of the chief speakers, who was a Communistic (sic) registered primary candidate for the school board, and who in filing her expense account as required by law, acknowledged that her expenses had been payed by the Alameda County Communist Party, urged the election of the five left-wing candidates for the City Council . . .

The paper used such terms as "the Doubtful Five" and "left-wing communists" in its news columns to refer to the five challengers.

But the "Doubtful Five" all won a plurality of votes in the April nominating election, qualifying for the runoff election. Their success was due to the organizing effort of the united labor groups, joined by the Oakland Voters League (OVL). Among other techniques the league mounted a giant torchlight parade. The Negro Labor Committee made a large float which showed AFL and CIO pallbearers lowering a casket labeled The Machine into the ground, while it portrayed the gloved fists of Oakland voters knocking the Tribune Tower in half. The slogan on the float read simply: "Let's finish the job—take the power out of the Tower." When the final votes were cast, the labor candidates had very nearly accomplished their aim: only one of the "Doubtful Five," Joe Goldfarb, the only one with a Jewish-sounding name, was defeated, and he by less than 1000 votes. The other four challengers all won by over 5000 votes, a margin of about 5 percent of the total of 97,520 votes cast. It was a comfortable margin.[30]

The program which the Five had run on included four main points which were repeated and expanded at a mass meeting in August following their election. The meeting was attended by over 200 delegates and observers from various labor locals, the Democratic party, and the Oakland Council of Churches. After discussing Oakland's problems at a day-long session, the group approved the following demands:

1. Draft a new city charter. "Scrap the old one with 231 amendments to the original sections."
2. Repeal the city sales tax; increase assessments of downtown

property owners; fire the county auditor; make the auditorship a
city office.

3. Call for city council neutrality during strikes in Oakland; repeal
the antipicketing and antihandbill ordinances.

4. Create a civic unity commission to enforce equality in city
employment and the administration of public welfare.

5. Maintain local rent control, build more local public housing, and
demand immediate aid in this activity from the state government
in Sacramento.

6. Examine the possibility of bypassing the Key System railway,[31]
and establish a publicly owned transport system in Alameda
County.

7. Overhaul the public health service from top to bottom, beginning
with the employment of enough public health nurses to bring
Oakland up to standards for cities its size.

8. Begin spending the $15 million authorized by the 1945 bond
issue for public schools; start building "the swimming pools that
were promised and the library that has been talked about for 20
years."

None of the OVL's platform, it might be noted, included bringing
more industry to Oakland, the major approach to city problems of the
Tribune, city managers, and private elites. (See Chapter Seven). It was
this platform, couched in terms of an attack on the *Tribune,* that had
brought four of the five challengers to victory. And, it could be argued,
that victory was in large part a repudiation of the politics and policies
of the preceding 15 years.[32]

As of June 1947, with the new councilmen seated, the city council
was in a precarious balance (five to four) in favor of the *Tribune* and
the "old politics." The OVL had failed to win a clear majority, and on
May 14 the *Tribune* had breathed an editorial sigh of relief: "Four new
council members were elected and one incumbent retained, with the
result that unless unlooked for changes in membership occur, the
majority control will rest in the hands of the present administration for
the next two years. This prevents drastic changes in city government."
The editorial had concluded: "The new members of the city council are
entitled to fair treatment and to aid and assistance from the public."

Within two weeks, the 5-4 balance had crystallized, so that the old council majority remained in control and Mr. Hassler remained as City Manager. Two years later a recall petition, originated by the Oakland Real Estate Board, succeeded in recalling one of the challengers, Scott Weakley, who later accused local employers of blackballing him and shortly thereafter committed suicide. The labor coalition, which had been the basis of the 1947 platform, fell apart, and by 1951 all the challengers had died or been defeated at the polls. Thus the dynamics of the 1946 upheaval played themselves out.

This experience of labor revolt is of considerable importance for any theory of local politics. The OVL had been the focus of a labor-centered coalition, as opposed to the party-centered, or executive-centered, coalition, which Robert Dahl speaks of in *Who Governs?*, or the *Tribune*-centered coalition which had ruled Oakland since 1941. It had raised again all the important issues which had been settled, more or less to the satisfaction of the business community, by the charters of 1911 and 1931—the charter form, franchises, and the control of the city manager—plus the new issues of housing and public-serving health and transportation systems which earlier charter fights had not considered. This set of demands represented what we might call a genuine electoral pluralism, because it offered a broad set of alternatives across a wide range of social and political issues, with each alternative oriented toward the needs of the working and middle classes of Oakland society. In short this was a powerful reform movement which aimed, not at the expropriation of corporate wealth, but at the redirection of the city's policies and policy beneficiaries.

But the OVL did not win. Moreover the circumstances which brought it together, a general strike and unity of all of labor's forces, were unusual. The degree of protest and objection to the city's postwar policies in many areas we will consider in subsequent chapters. But the failure of the OVL, and the inability of black organizations in the 1960s and early 1970s to win in local elections, has meant that the *Tribune's* coalition continues today to control the election of mayor, council majority, and (since a majority chooses the manager) the city manager himself. Far from exiting from city politics, the corporate-political coalition has been able to withstand, over a period of 25 years of city history, all challenges to its domination of the electoral process. The context of political combat and policy making since 1947 has been set by that basic fact of political power.

NOTES

1. For a recent analysis of how corporate ownership affects reporting about the activities of corporations, see Herbert I. Schiller, "Mind Management: Mass Media in the Advanced Industrial State," *Quarterly Review of Economics and Business,* Spring 1971, pp. 39-52.
2. Accepted not only by the wealthy but by the non affluent as well. See Helen and Robert Lynd, *Middletown in Transition,* New York: Harcourt, Brace, 1937, pp. 444 ff; Ely Chinoy, *The Automobile Workers and the American Dream,* Boston: Beacon Press, 1955, chap. 1; and Robert Lane, *Political Ideology, Why the American Common Man Believes the Way He Does,* New York: MacMillan, 1962, pp. 254 ff.
3. This can be analyzed as an aspect of the mobilized bias of the political system that is discussed by Peter Bachrach and Morton Baratz in *Power and Poverty, Theory and Practice,* New York: Oxford University, 1970, esp. chap. 1.
4. This point has been made recently by Patricia and Kenneth Dolbeare: "The two are mutually supportive belief systems, however, for each makes sometimes unstated assumptions about the other. For example, capitalism assumes a government of limited powers which practices laissez-faire policies. Liberalism constructs such a government because it assumes the effective working of the capitalist economic system, particularly the free and competitive market." From *American Ideologies, Competing Political Beliefs of the 1970s,* Chicago: Markham, 1971, p. 48. See also Richard Edgar, *Urban Power and Social Welfare, Corporate Influence in an American City,* Beverly Hills: Sage, 1971, chap. 2.
5. For the history of the city and this early land giveaway, see: M. W. Wood, *History of Alameda County,* Oakland: Pacific Press, 1938, pp. 488-489; Dr. Peter Conmy, (Oakland City Librarian), *The Beginnings of Oakland, California, A.U.C.,* Oakland: The Oakland Public Library, 1961, pp. 19 ff; and William Wilcox Robinson, *Land In California,* Berkeley and Los Angeles: University of California, 1948.
6. The estimated value added by manufacturers is 40 percent of total value, the same ratio as obtained for the city in 1939. Value added is not listed by the Census of Manufacturers for 1925. The sources of data are *Census of Manufacturers, 1939,* vol. 3; *Census of Manufacturers, 1925.*
7. In 1954 the census began using a new category, "value added by manufacturer—*adjusted,*" which increased the total figure by about 30 percent over the unadjusted figure used in earlier censuses. The figure used here for 1967 is the adjusted figure, the only category the census still uses. The sources of these data are *Census of Manufacturers, 1958,* vol. 3, and *Census . . . 1967,* vol. 3.
8. Sherman Maisel, *Housebuilding in Transition,* Berkeley and Los Angeles: University of California, 1953, p. 23.
9. John Herzog, *An Analysis of the Dynamics of Large-Scale Housebuilding,*

unpublished Ph.D. dissertation, University of California, Berkeley, School of Business Administration, 1962, p. 39.

10. Maisel, op. cit., p. 68.

11. Some examples: Robert Dahl, *Who Governs?* New Haven: Yale University, 1961, bk.I; "The Bifurcation of Power in a Satellite City," in Morris Janowitz, ed., *Community Power Systems,* Glencoe, Ill.: Free Press, 1961. Michael Aiken and Paul Mott, eds., *The Structure of Community Power,* New York: Random House, 1970, *passim*; and Willis Hawley and Fred Wirt, *The Search for Community Power,* New York, Prentice-Hall, 1968, *passim.*

12. As this early example makes clear, corporate influence is not necessarily monolithic, and certainly was not 70 years ago. However, on statewide issues Pardee was pro-railroad, and the Southern Pacific later endorsed him for governor: "In 1902 George C. Pardee, the (Southern Pacific) railroad's candidate for governor, was elected." Loren Mowry, *The California Progressives,* Berkeley: University of California, 1951, p. 20.

13. For an excellent historical presentation of the growth and decline of Socialist party national and urban strength, see James Weinstein, *The Decline of Socialism in America,* New York: Vintage Books, 1967, chap. 2.

14. Edgar J. Hinkel and William E. McCann, *Oakland, 1852-1938: Some Phases of the Social, Political, and Economic History of Oakland, California,* under the auspices of Works Progress Administration (Oakland Public Library, 1939), vol. 2, p. 765.

15. *American City,* October 1911, p. 225.

16. The devastating effects of nonpartisanship and at-large provisions of the commission charters on the Socialist party in several American cities is analyzed by James Weinstein, "Organized Business and the City Commission and Manager Movements," *Journal of Southern History,* May 1962, pp. 166-182; and Samuel P. Hays, "The Politics of Reform in Municipal Government in the Progressive Era," *Pacific Northwest Quarterly,* October 1964, pp. 157-169.

17. The *Tribune* refused to print any news of the investigation, apparently outraged that city bluebloods should be implicated. But the San Francisco papers carried the full story.

18. As quoted in *Oakland Tribune.*

19. In 1930 the *Tribune* printed at least eight articles which favored the amendments, the *Inquirer* at least a dozen. See *Tribune* editorial, September 16, 1930.

20. The main facts in this section are drawn from Amelia R. Fry, "Conservation and Politics, An Interview with Joseph R. Knowland," University of California, Regional Oral History Project, 1965, p. ii.

21. See Harold Ickes, *America's House of Lords, An Inquiry into Freedom of the Press,* New York: Harcourt, 1939, pp. 141-143. Ickes also made his case in *Time* magazine, August 14, 1939. Knowland strongly objected to Ickes' allegations.

22. The others are the Los Angeles *Times* and the San Francisco *Chronicle* and the Copley-owned papers in San Diego.

23. Interview with Richard C. Hamb, March 25, 1968.

24. Interview with Peter G. Conmy, Oakland Librarian, March 1968.

25. See Herbert Resner, *The Law in Action during the San Francisco Longshore and Maritime Strike of 1934*, Berkeley: Works Progress Administration, 1936 (typewritten, located in University of California, Berkeley, documents library), pp. 125-126.

26. See A. M. Rosenson, *The CIO Movement in Alameda County,* unpublished Master's thesis (Economics), University of California, Berkeley, 1937, chap. 1.

27. F. H. Douma, *The Oakland General Strike,* unpublished Master's thesis (Economics), University of California, Berkeley, 1951, p. 76.

28. The only other serious challenge to the paper's hegemony has been raised by the Oakland Black Caucus, organized in the 1960's. But even the caucus has been unable to elect any candidate to the city council, much less a majority. For an analysis of the caucus see Chapter Seven, pp. 154-155.

29. Many of the facts in the following pages about the General Strike are drawn from Douma, op. cit.

30. Substantial irregularities were reported during election day. In West Oakland an OVL poll watcher complained to the city clerk that the election officials in his precinct were not checking off names of those who had already voted. The clerk took no reported action. On election day 14 OVL precinct workers were arrested by Oakland police and charged with distributing handbills outside a union meeting without a permit. One of the challenger candidates, Scott Weakley, made an angry protest over a local radio station and rallied the remaining election workers to "ignore the police drive." When labor attorneys reached the police station the 14 workers were released and all charges dropped. (CIO) *Labor Herald,* July 15, 1947, p. 3.

31. The Key System was the Eastbay's interurban rail system which connected Berkeley, Oakland, and other Eastbay cities. Key also ran a train across the Bay Bridge to San Francisco until the early 1960s.

32. Peter Bachrach's analysis of Baltimore provides a cogent framework for interpretation of the 1947 Oakland elections. The mobilization of bias in Oakland was a political system which, until 1947, had eliminated every Populist and Democratic politician from local politics and which the voters repudiated by electing four of five candidates pledged to draw up a new charter and provide significant public services. See Bachrach and Baratz, op. cit., esp. chaps. 1 and 3.

CHAPTER TWO

Power and Decision:
The Political System

In this chapter we shall examine some structural and quantifiable elements of political rule in the city, and devise a set of certain basic factors which have given shape to the city's politics since the new charter of 1930. These factors show direct political participation in city politics. as opposed to indirect political rule. Indirect political rule simply refers to the extent to which the ruling stratum in Oakland politics has taken into account the wishes and interests of individuals and classes not directly represented in the ruling stratum. In his book, *Who Governs?*, Professor Dahl, in speaking about the indirect influence of voters over public officials, emphasizes that government officials, while they are selected from the middle classes, still represent, to a substantial degree, the wishes of groups and individuals not directly engaged in decision making.[1] This argument is consistent with the Marxist argument that the United States, and its cities, is governed by a ruling class; since a ruling-class stratum is *always* responsive, to some extent, to the wishes of the public, if it wants to remain in rule and not be overthrown. It is when government is forced to choose, in policy making and enforcement, between upper and lower classes that we might see its alleged class nature. Similarly, "class rule" would be suggested if the political system's decision makers are recruited on a consistent basis from the same, and narrowly defined, social groups or classes; or if the mechanism of selection of decision makers closely controlled at an elite level.[2] To measure the extent of the latter two criteria in Oakland we present the following evidence: voting turnout in city elections; county party registration, compared to party registration of elected officials; election versus appointments as an avenue to seats on the city council; the group and class affiliations of all appointments to city offices over a 5-year period; and the professional backgrounds of the city's mayors and city managers since 1871. Together these data provide us with a fairly rounded picture of the extent of limitation on democracy in the city.

Voting turnout for the city council elections is shown in Tables 2-1 and 2-2.

The voting turnout between 1949 and 1963 is shown in Table 2-2. As can be seen from a comparison of Tables 2-1 and 2-2, voting turnout is quite low (compared to presidential or even state turnouts) in each of the periods studied. These figures show only the percent of *registered* voters voting, and so err to some extent by making the turnout seem larger than it would be if the figures measured the percent of voting age citizens voting. In part the increase in the postwar voting pattern reflects the intense political campaigns of 1947-1951 between organized labor and the *Tribune*. Yet the fact that less than half of even the registered voters vote in Oakland elections, on the average, suggests that

TABLE 2-1 Percentage of registered voters voting in Oakland by highest, lowest, and average vote turnout, 1931-1945

Highest	47.90%	1933 nominating election
Lowest	19.75	1937 general election
Average*	31.30	

*For both nominating and general elections combined.

TABLE 2-2 Percentage of registered voters voting in Oakland by highest, lowest, and average vote turnout, 1947-1963

Highest	53.90%	1961 nominating election
Lowest	29.80	1953 general election
Average*	40.80	

*For both nominating and general elections combined.

only 20 percent of the city electorate is needed to elect a city councilman. This provides a very limited mandate for any elected city official.

In Table 2-3 are shown the number of votes cast in the highest, lowest, and average voter turnouts in city elections since 1947. Taking half the average number of votes cast as the figure necessary for winning an election, we arrive at a figure of 37,400 votes. If the city's councilmen were elected from seven districts, as the small businessmen have demanded twice, the number of votes necessary to winning a council seat would be reduced to 5,343. In contested elections, costs can easily rise to $1.00 per vote. This would mean that a contested election within the citywide election system would cost each candidate $37,400; within the ward, or district, system, $5,343. This explains the interest of small businessmen in returning to the ward system. It does not explain, however, the willingness of one recent council candidate to pay $34,000 for a council seat which pays incumbents around $30 a week, or $1,400 a year, for attendance at regular meetings.

County registration figures also tell us something about representativeness and direct rule on the city council in recent decades. These figures are given in Table 2-4. While the party registration of registered

TABLE 2-3   *Number of votes cast in Oakland, 1947-1963*

High	95,490	1961 nominating and bond election
Low	58,226	1957 general election
Average*	74,800	

*For both nominating and general elections combined.

TABLE 2-4   *Party registration, Alameda County, 1930-1960*

Year	%Democratic	%Republican	%other
1930	16.2	78.9	4.9
1940	54.8	41.9	3.3
1950	57.6	38.6	3.8
1960	60.0	36.7	3.4

Source: Eugene C. Lee, *California Votes 1938-1960,* Berkeley: Institute of Governmental Studies, University of California, 1963, pp. A-30, A-35, A-40, and A-45.

voters in Alameda County swung from very heavily Republican to heavily Democratic in the three decades 1930-1960, the Oakland city council made no such wide change in party affiliation. The New Deal slate which tried for office in 1937 was defeated, and no similar attempt was made until 1947. In this latter year, three of the four labor candidates were Democrats (and the remaining one, a "decline to state"), but the last of them was defeated in 1951. Not until the late 1950s did Democrats begin to turn up on the city council in significant numbers, although still in a minority. In good measure the nonpartisanship provision, which hurt the Socialist party after 1911, has retarded the Democratic party in recent years. Had Democrats won the same percentage in local as they won inside the city in partisan (state and Federal) races, they would have won 10 more seats and held a majority on the Oakland council by 1965.[3]

TABLE 2-5 *Avenues by which non-incumbents won office in Oakland City Council, 1933-1965*

Appointment of non-incumbent	21
Following death of incumbent	10
Prior to elections, no death	3
Election of non-incumbent	22*
Since 1941	17
Tribune-endorsed, since 1941	11†
Election of non-incumbent as a percentage of total council electoral races	29
Election of incumbent as percentage of total council electoral races	71

Source: From printed endorsements of the Oakland *Tribune*.

Note: There were a total of 76 council races, which includes 1949 recall elections of three of the four labor candidates elected in 1947, and special race to fill the seat of one so recalled, on February 28, 1950 (counted as four races).

*Includes election of four anti-Carr councilmen in 1933 election. This category refers simply to the election of non-incumbents (incumbent not necessarily running).

†Candidates winning election of council without *Tribune* endorsement, 1941-1965, include only the following: the four labor candidates, in 1947 and after; John W. Holmdahl, 1955; Robert L. Osborn, 1957, 1961, 1965; Howard Rilea, 1965.

Another way of looking at power is to examine the methods by which city councilmen have arrived in office. Table 2-5 shows how new councilmen have arrived on the council between 1933 and 1965, and the position of the Oakland *Tribune* on candidates winning office by election during these years. Of the 21 appointments to office shown in Table 2-5, 18 occurred during councils which had a conservative, *Tribune*-supported majority. One of these appointments, John Houlihan, not atypical in politics or background among other appointees, later became the *Tribune's* strongly endorsed candidate for mayor. Houlihan had at one time successfully defended the paper against a libel suit. Of the appointed category, these 18 can be considered friendly to the newspaper and a part of the ruling coalition. Only five candidates between 1941 and 1965 won election to city council more than once without *Tribune* support.

What Table 2-5 also shows is the large number of appointments to office—almost 50 percent of all new councilmen for the years studied acquired office originally through appointment. The ability of incumbents to remain in office is also clear from the table. Well over two-thirds of all races were won by incumbents. The record of numerous appointments to council, high victory ratio of incumbents, and the failure of non-*Tribune* endorsed candidates to reach office indicates a pattern of elitism in local politics in Oakland.

Still another index of the elements of power within the ruling stratum is obtained by tracing the organizational affiliations of public officeholders. Table 2-6 shows the economic and group affiliations of all appointees to all city offices during the six years 1961 to 1966, inclusive.[4]

Table 2-6 shows the limited ideological and social base of appointments to public office. Very few members of neighborhood associations or poor people's organizations were appointed to city office. The Oakland Chamber of Commerce lists 147 business associations either headquartered or doing business in Oakland.[5] These range from Bay Area-wide groups, such as the Administrative Management Society, National, Oakland-East Bay Chapter, to associations whose activity is strictly limited to an Oakland constituency, such as the Downtown Merchants Parking Association. Only somewhat over 20 business associations are represented in the appointments shown in Table 2-6, and these appointments come almost exclusively from business groups (such as the chamber of commerce, the most heavily represented single group

TABLE 2-6   Group and class affiliation of all appointments to city council, boards, and commissions, 1961-1966

Business	
Sierra Club	3
Traders Club	3
Chamber of commerce	6
Real estate board	2
Business association	6
Junior chamber	2
Total	22
Service, fraternal	
Knights of Columbus	1
Rotary, Lion, Kiwanis	7
United Crusade	6
Elks, Moose	3
Native Sons of the Golden West	1
Masons	5
League of Women Voters	1
Lake Merritt Breakfast Club	2
PTA, Dads' Club	2
College fraternity	2
OCCUR	2
Total	32
Social	
Athens Athletic Club	4
Athenian Nile Club	4
Museum, symphony associations	5
Total	13
Poor, middle-income, black	
NAACP, Men of Tomorrow	3
District councils	3
Improvement associations	1
Total	7
Labor, professional	
Central Labor Council	3
Union official	3
Lawyers' association	1
Total	7
GRAND TOTAL	81

Source: Compiled from biographies of candidates for appointment, as submitted to mayor of Oakland. On file, mayor's office, Oakland, California.

in the whole of Table 2-6) which are strictly limited to an Oakland constituency. The Oakland Chamber also lists 111 cultural and avocational groups, ranging from the Art League of the East Bay to the Young People's Symphony Orchestra Association.[6] Yet only two such groups, the museum association and the Oakland Symphony Association, were represented in appointive office from 1961 to 1966, the five persons shown in Table 2-6. The Oakland Chamber lists 26 improvement associations,[7] the majority of which are from middle- and upper-middle income areas of the city. Yet only one improvement association was represented in the appointments recorded in Table 2-6. In short, if we leave aside for the moment labor unions and simply examine the business, cultural, and improvement groups listed as operating in Oakland by the chamber of commerce, the city had a total of 284 possible groups from which to appoint members of the city council. In fact it made its selections from only 38 nonlabor groups. The implication of these figures is that, while Oakland may bear out de Tocqueville's comments that America is a highly organized society, nevertheless there is only a very small fraction of the total of even middle-class and business organizations which hold power. Labor and the poor are not the only elements of society which are included out.

Table 2-6 also shows that business dominates the list of appointees. They hold all the positions under the business category in Table 2-6; they are easily the predominant force in the organizations in the service and fraternal category. They also predominate in the social category, since the clientele of both the Athens Athletic Club and the Athenian Nile Club is predominantly business. Thus at least half, and probably a greater proportion, of the 84 group and class affiliations are with business groups.

Thus within what is already a quite limited number of represented groups, business and business-predominant affiliations comprise the overwhelming majority.

Still another method of measuring the unrepresentativeness of the ruling stratum is to examine the professional occupations of Oakland's mayors. Dahl found that New Haven's mayors were almost entirely businessmen and manufacturers between 1842 and 1897, and that after this period a succession of lawyers and businessmen (and one labor executive) served as mayor up to 1953. In 1953 Richard Lee, previously the director of the Yale University news bureau, became mayor. In contrast, Oakland does not show even the transition to a white-collar professional mayor, but continues its century-old pattern of business mayors today, as is shown in Table 2-7.

Of the 24 mayors appearing in Table 2-7, 12 have been in business (including banking), 6 have been lawyers, 4 have been professionals other than lawyers, 1 was a worker, and 1 a government employee. Thus the mayoralty, the most important single elective office in the city, is an area of direct rule of businessmen and lawyers.

The office of city manager is perhaps of equal importance to the office of mayor as a center of policy making and execution. Can we find the same pattern of *direct* business rule in this office?

Oakland has had, since 1933, a total of five city managers. The first manager, O. E. Carr, had been manager in other cities before coming to Oakland in 1931; his selection was worked out in advance by the *Tribune* and active political groups, and he was honored by a reception upon his arrival in town at the Knowland-founded Oakland Athletic Club. Ousted in 1933, he shortly became an official in a securities investment firm and in 1959 made a gift of $500,000 to his college. The second manager, John Hassler, (1933-1943; 1946-1954), a high official at a leading local bank, held the office longer than any other

TABLE 2-7   *Professional occupations of Oakland's mayors, 1876-1968*

E. H. Pardee, 1876-1878
Physician

James E. Blethen, 1880-1882
Carpenter, East Oakland Planing Mills

Charles K. Robinson 1882-1883
Businessman, S. Martin and Company

J. West Martin, 1883-1884
President, Union Savings Bank

A. C. Davis, 1887-1888
Lawyer(?) Davis and Hill

C. D. Pierce, 1888-1889
General hardware and manufacturers' agent

John R. Glascock, 1889-1891
Lawyer

Melvin C. Chapman, 1891-1893
Lawyer

TABLE 2-7 (Continued)

George C. Pardee, 1893-1895
Occulist and aurist, Oakland and San Francisco offices

John L. Davie, 1895-1897
John L. Davie Transportation Co.

W. R. Thomas, 1897-1899
Real estate, Benham and Thomas

Roland W. Show, 1899-1901
Wholesale hardware

Anson Barstow, 1901-1903
Wood, Coal, Hay and Grain

Warren Olney, 1903-1905
Layer

Frank K. Mott, 1905-1915
Hardware store owner

John L. Davie, 1915-1930
President, John L. Davie Transportation Co.

Fred N. Morcom, 1931-1933
Art goods

Dr. William J. McCracken, 1933-1941
Dentist

Dr. John F. Slavich, 1941-1945
Physician and surgeon

Herbert L. Beach, 1945-1947
President and General Manager, Beach-Krahn Amusement Co.

Joseph E. Smith, 1947-1949
Smith and Parrish, Attorneys

Clifford E. Rishell, 1949-1961
Signpainter

John C. Houlihan, 1961-1966
Lawyer

John Reading, 1966--
President, Ingrams Food Products

Main sources: Hustead and Polks City Directories for Oakland, 1876
to date.

manager; and was roundly praised by the local employers and de-
nounced by labor for his handling of the General Strike in 1946. The
city's third manager, Charles Schwanenberg, (1943-1946) came from
the presidency of a leading local department store. The fourth manager,
Wayne Thompson (1955-1965), was a Kaiser industries employee before becoming manager, and stated frankly the dependency of the city
on public and business leaders for the success of a major government
project (see p. 147); he is now vice-president of Dayton Department
Stores, a large chain in Minnesota. The incumbent manager, Jerome
Keithley, (1965-   ) coming from a manager position in another California city where the city had owned the electric utility, has never
suggested city ownership of utilities in Oakland. All manager appointments have had direct or indirect approval of the *Tribune,* since a
manager is appointed by a city council majority and the *Tribune*
coalition dominates council elections. Hence, while several managers
have been professional managers and not businessmen, their method of
selection and need of private support for projects keeps them closely
attuned to the city business establishment's point of view. And at least
two have retired to high-paying positions in the business world.

POLICE AND THE POWER STRUCTURE

Most studies of community power have overlooked the question of
police behavior as a major indicator of who rules, of the distribution of
political power in society. The question of the social-class background
of decision makers, like mayors and city managers, is of no greater
importance in the' scheme of local power than the question of how the
legal violence of the policeman's gun and club is used, and whether it is
used partially or impartially.

Frequently, police force has been directed against unions. As Philip
Taft and Philip Ross have written, the United States has had the
bloodiest and most violent labor history of any industrial nation in the
world; before World War I "armed troops were usually employed once
labor disputes became seriously disruptive," while during the single year
1936 state troops were called out 11 times in connection with labor
disputes. Labor charges of brutality against police were common in

those days. After 10 pickets were shot and killed by police at the south Chicago plant of Republic Steel Corporation in 1937, a United States Senate committee found that:

"The provocation for the police assault did not go beyond abusive language and throwing of isolated missiles from the rear ranks of the marchers. . . . From all the evidence we think it plain that the force employed by the police was far in excess of that which the occasion required."[8]

And Richard Maxwell Brown writes that "The modern urban police system was created in reaction to the riots of the 1830s, 1840s, and 1850s."[9]

It is clear from these and other known chapters of American labor history that one function of police is to weaken or eliminate the unions' power of strike, and thereby maximize the employer's control over the functioning of the plants. In Oakland, the police have followed this national pattern. In the decades of labor militancy, the police have acted as a control mechanism against political insurgency and as defenders of property rights. During the mid-thirties a professor of political science at the University of California, David P. Barrows, led a detachment of the National Guard to put down the San Francisco longshoremen's strike.[10] And we have detailed the activity of the Oakland police during the General Strike in 1946.

The activity of the police as expressions of the legal violence of the state is crucial to an understanding of power: who is satisfied, and who dissatisfied, with police behavior tells us a good deal about how power is used in the city. And in Oakland we find a general satisfaction with police practices on the part of the local newspaper and business establishment, and a continued dissatisfaction with their practices by militant blacks, and by some local labor officials who find that police still enforce the right to cross picket lines more than the right to strike. None of the half-dozen labor officials I talked with between 1965 and 1968 viewed the police as friendly; at best the police were viewed as "neutral against strikes." Yet the city newspaper refrained from any editorial criticism of the police, even when shots fired from a police car riddled the front windows of the Black Panther headquarters in 1968.[11] Clearly the county's labor unions do not dominate police policy. During the General Strike, direct business pressure was visibly and forcefully brought on the police chief and city manager. But the pattern of influence of the city's businessmen over police activity is generally indirect. The police force is subject to direction and criticism from the chief in a climate of opinion heavily influenced by the *Tribune;* and none of these parties in recent years has been in the least symphatetic to labor or militant black organizing.

The problem of racial attitudes has also been substantial on the city's police force. According to Professor Jerome Skolnick, whose book *Justice Without Trial* considers the Oakland police in depth and is generally sympathetic toward the Oakland force, "A negative attitude toward Negroes was a norm among the police studied, as recognized by the chief himself. If a policeman did not subscribe to it, unless a Negro himself, he would be somewhat resented by his fellows."[12]

In 1965, just before Skolnick's book length study of the Oakland police was published by a major publisher, the chief of Oakland's police issued an order to all employees of the department, forbidding use of the words, boy, spade, jig, nigger, blue, smoke, coon, etc. Yet apparently this directive was not enough, since in the same year several incidents erupted, including one in which a Negro man picketed the police building for seven weeks, claiming he had been assaulted in his house by police officers;[13] the next year two Oakland patrolmen were fired for beating a prisoner "with their fists," after arresting him in the Negro section of West Oakland.[14] The Black Panthers, who originated in Oakland, began as an armed patrol to insure that blacks were treated lawfully by the police; and their own experience in the Oakland jails has been harsh.[15] Finally, most of the Panther leadership has been jailed or forced into exile; the internal split in the party, between Newton on the West Coast and Seale in the East, can be attributed to the heavy pressure which the national government, as well as the Oakland police, has put on Panther leaders.

Not all of the violence shown black political leaders is simply the result of racial attitudes of the police. The violence and harassment complained of by union organizers in the 1930s and 1940s was equally great;[16] Panthers have simply encountered the police attitude of hostility toward any group moving militantly for socialism or for increased power for the powerless. But there is also the added factor of racial attitudes in cases of police behavior towards nonwhites. In 1935 the Harlem Riot Commission Report sharply critized "police aggression" against Harlem; a 1966 report to the United States President's Commission on Law Enforcement found that 72 percent of police officers in three large Northern cities expressed "extreme" or "considerable" prejudice toward nonwhites, while the 1961 Report on Justice of the U.S. Commission on Civil Rights concluded that "Police brutality . . . is a serious problem in the United States."[17]

Racial attitudes have also been a serious problem in Oakland. Many of the city's police have been recruited in the Deep South, and all have been white. One of these was Lester Divine, who became chief of the Oakland police in May of 1949. During his period in office the number of cases of police brutality increased considerably, and in January of 1950, less than a year after Divine assumed office, the California State Assembly Interim Committee on Crime and Corrections held a full investigation into the practices of the Oakland police force, the first and only time that such a state investigation has been held in California. While 28 Oakland police officers took the stand to deny all brutality charges, the majority of the remaining 31 witnesses emphatically asserted charges all the way from needless arm twisting and name calling to the shooting by an Oakland policeman on an unemployed cannery worker in the worker's own house. Chief Divine admitted the practice of holding persons for 72 hours for "investigation" without filing charges. "All Police Departments do it," he said.[18] Under Wyman Vernon, who succeeded Divine in February 1955 as chief of police, brutality charges subsided. Under Chief Edward Toothman (1959-1966) the charges of brutality, including charges of shooting suspects in the back, arose again.

Thus charges of harassment have varied substantially in Oakland depending on who the chief of police is, but one factor has remained constant throughout the periods of severe police harassment: many of the victims have been Negro, including the cannery worker who was shot in his own house.

CONCLUSIONS

What does the evidence on the political stratum and police behavior tell us about who has ruled the city's government since 1931? While the data are diverse, a broad pattern does emerge:

1. Concerning the professional background or group affiliation of city councilmen, mayors' recent appointments to office, and city managers, the great majority are businessmen, either before, during, or after their terms of public office.

2. The occupations of current appointees to city government follows very closely the occupational patterns of mayors in the last century.

3. The city council has been substantially separated from the social and political views of the majority of Oakland voters. The discrepancy between councilmen's political party registration and prevailing party registration and voting trends in the city and county, and the occupational background of city officials, shows that the city's administrations have been conducted by those who are in a minority position as measured by the above indexes.

4. The police have served constantly to protect the interests of local property owners. At the same time, police have acted to control or limit the insurgent power of labor or blacks in general, although recent activity has been aimed most heavily against the Panthers while allowing more moderate black groups, those still willing to work within the system, relative freedom from harassment.

5. Given the fact of a one-newspaper town, the ability of incumbents to retain office, the charter system of at-large elections and nonpartisanship, and the hostile behavior of police toward labor and black organizers, electoral politics has been highly limited in its conceptive aspects, and successful community organizing for change has been impeded. Oakland displays a pattern of political elitism and class rule, rather than pluralism, in that the election of public officials is controlled from the top, the social basis of recruitment of both elected and administrative officials is limited to the middle class or business, and the police forces of the city have been consistently used to protect the power position both of the business community and of the city government itself.

NOTES

1. Robert Dahl, *Who Governs?* New Haven: Yale University, 1961, pp. 163-165.
2. Articles arguing the meaning, and existence, of class rule in America are legion. Only a few are here noted. Arguing that there is class rule are the following: G. William Domhoff, *Who Rules America?*, Englewood Cliffs, N.J.: Prentice-Hall, 1967; Paul M. Sweezy, "Power Elite or Ruling Class?" *Monthly Review,* September 1956; Herbert Aptheker, "Power in America," *Mainstream,* September 1956. The last two articles and several others on both sides of the issue are to be found in G. William Domhoff and Hoyt B. Ballard, eds., *C. Wright Mills and the Power Elite,* Boston: Beacon Press, 1968. Arguing against the existence of such rule are, notably, Nelson Polsby, *Community Power and Political Theory,* New Haven: Yale University, 1963.
3. My thanks to Dr. Willis Hawley for this insight.
4. The total number of appointments during the period represented by Table 2-6 was 35. The total of group and class affiliations (81) exceeds the number of appointees because most appointees had two or more group memberships, while the concepts "class affiliation" and "group affiliation" are overlapping.
5. Oakland, Chamber of Commerce, "Business-Trade-Professional Organizations, March 1966-1967,"
6. Oakland Chamber of Commerce, "Cultural and Avocation Groups, March 1966-1967."
7. Oakland Chamber of Commerce, "Improvement Associations, June 1966-1967."
8. Philip Taft and Philip Ross, "American Labor Violence: Its Causes, Character, and Outcome," in Hugh Graham and Ted Gurr, eds., *The History of Violence in America,* New York: Bantam, 1969, p. 359.
9. Maxwell Brown, "Historical Patterns of Violence in America," in Graham and Gurr, op. cit., p. 54.
10. See Herbert Resner, *The Law in Action,* Berkeley: Works Progress Administration, 1936, p. 122 and passim.
11. The two policemen to whom the car was assigned were on duty at the time and "roaring drunk"; they denied any responsibility for the incident but were suspended from the force, arrested, and released on $3,000 bail. Gene Marine, *The Black Panthers,* New York: Signet Books, 1969, p. 183.
12. Jerome Skolnick, *Justice Without Trial: Law Enforcement in a Democratic Society,* New York: Wiley, 1966, p. 81. In general Skolnick's book provides almost no support for complaints of police brutality.
13. Mr. Luther Smith never received satisfaction from the courts for what he described as an unprovoked attack on himself and his family. A full account is in Amory Bradford, *Oakland's Not for Burning,* New York: McKay, 1968, pp. 131-140.
14. Oakland *Tribune* March 7, 1967, p. 1.
15. See Bobby Seale, *Seize the Time; The Story of the Black Panther Party and Huey P. Newton,* New York: Random House, 1970.

16. Complaints by organized labor against the police can be found in: (Communist Party) *Western Worker,* March 6, 1933; April 10, 1933; December 11, 1933; September 9, 1935; September 26, 1935; September 14, 1936; February 8, 1937; and also in the (AFL) *East Bay Labor Journal,* January 29, 1937; and California (CIO), *Labor Herald,* June 22, 1937; and June 15, 1938.

17. In Jerome Skolnick, *The Politics of Protest, A Report to the National Commission on the Causes and Prevention of Violence,* New York, Ballantine Books, 1969, pp. 243-244.

18. San Francisco *Chronicle,* January 5, 1950, p. 16. Testimony at the hearing, and background articles, are to be found in the following: San Francisco *Chronicle* January 6, 1950, p. 3; January 7, 1950, p. 1; Oakland *Tribune* January 4, 1950, p. 21; January 5, 1950, p. 7; January 6, 1950, p. 2; and *People's World,* January 3, 4, and 5, 1950.

CHAPTER THREE

The Functioning of the Urban Economy

Chapter One dealt with the evolving structure of Oakland's corporate economy, and the potential which that evolution has given the urban business sector for effective political activity. Chapter Two has shown the realization of that potential by a highly political newspaper, drawing on the potential of its monopoly status. In this chapter we will be looking at the economy again, but from the point of view of the economy's own decision process and its inability to perform certain supply functions. Specifically we will be looking at the questions of, first, how well the city's corporate structure has supplied jobs, income, and housing to Oakland; second, how the decision structure and economic motive of the private economy has affected the supply of these commodities, and racial discrimination as an intrinsic part of the private decision process; and finally, the social consequences of this decision process. We begin with the functioning of the industrial system as a whole and will then look at the real estate industry.

THE ECONOMY AS SUPPLIER: JOBS, INCOME, AND POVERTY

This chapter views poverty as a phenomenon which results from the failures of the political and economic systems to provide an adequate supply of jobs and income to the community. While income can be increased marginally by increases in wage levels or job mobility, any major increases in income must come from a strong increase in the job supply and/or heavy transfer payments from government.[1] Hence this view of poverty, placing the initial blame in part on the failure of the economic system, provides us with a potent perspective for analyzing industrial performance.

Economists have long debated whether poverty and unemployment are the results of the system of private enterprise, or capitalism, that developed in the eighteenth and nineteenth centuries, or whether these problems are due to particular aspects of this economic system, subject to correction within the present economic framework. Surprisingly no studies of community power since the Lynds' study of Middletown have raised the problem of the connection between the urban political economy and poverty itself.[2] Yet a strong empirical case can be made that poverty, unemployment, and layoffs are always associated with the economy of early and modern capitalism, and that these kinds of economic problems are a necessary part of the economic system itself. The argument was made before Marx by the classical economist David Ricardo, who argued that the market mechanism could maintain the laboring classes of society at no better than subsistence, but defended the market system anyway as the most efficient mechanism for dis-

TABLE 3-1   Distribution of families by income in 1959—City of Oakland

	Families			
Annual income	Number	Percent	Number within levels	Percent within levels
Above deprivation				
$6,000 or more	51,927	53.4	51,927	53.4
Deprivation level				
under $6,000	45,266*	46.6*	21,115	21.8
Poverty level				
under $4,000	24,151*	24.8*	14,219	14.6
Extreme deprivation				
under $2,000	9,932	10.2	9,932	10.2
Total families			97,193	100.0

Source: Gene Bernardi, "Characteristics of the Spanish-Surname Population in the City of Oakland," *Oakland Interagency Project, 1965*, p. 7.
*Cumulative figure

tribution of goods.[3] Marx and neo-Marxists have created the most elaborated theory of this connection.[4] It seems, too, that the argument is admitted by mainstream American economists who discuss alleviating poverty and reducing unemployment to "acceptable" levels, but who rarely speak seriously about *eliminating* poverty in the United States, even when the 1972 level of American GNP exceeds $1 trillion. Thus there is some agreement between socialist and conservative economists that under the present system of political economy, economic hardship in the form of poverty for millions of people is an unavoidable part of life.

PEOPLE AT THE BOTTOM: OAKLAND'S POOR

For the city of Oakland in the 1960s the problem of poverty and deprivation was enormous, as it has been throughout most of this century. As the figures shown in Table 3-1 indicate, one-quarter of all families live in real poverty, at less than $4,000 a year; 46.6 percent—almost half of all families in the city—live in deprivation or worse. A total of 3,871 families and unrelated individuals earn less than $1,000 annually. Thus, in a time of major economic prosperity almost half the people of the city remain ill fed and ill housed. Unemployment is also widespread. In each of the years shown in Table 3-2, Oakland's rate has been at least 70 percent higher than that of the San Francisco-Oakland Standard Metropolitan Statistical Area (SMSA), and at least 50 percent higher than the state and national rates.

TABLE 3-2   Unemployment in United States, California, San Francisco-Oakland SMSA, and City of Oakland, 1959-1963

Year	United States	California	San Francisco-Oakland SMSA	Oakland
1959	5.5	4.8	4.6	8.5
1960	5.6	5.8	4.9	9.0
1961	6.7	6.9	5.8	10.7
1962	5.6	5.9	5.2	9.6
1963	5.7	6.0	5.3	9.7

Source: Mayor John C. Houlihan et al., *Over-all Economic Development Program*, Oakland, 1964(?), p. 7. The source cited by this study for the figures is the U.S. Department of Labor.

This burden of poverty falls heavily on the flatlands area, the poorest area, which borders the central business district. A study by the U.S. Department of Labor in 1966 shows that in that (flatlands) area the subemployment rate during the summer of 1966 was 30 percent. It found that exactly 60 percent of the area's residents were Negroes, and about 8 percent were Mexican-American. The total of unemployed, not looking for work, and subemployed in the flatlands according to this survey is a shocking 47 percent of the total work-eligible population, almost half the entire work force of the flatlands.[5] Figures for the city as a whole, including the non-flatlands areas, confirm this picture. As of 1960, the census showed 6.0 percent of all whites, 9.0 percent of all Spanish surname persons, and 13.8 percent of all nonwhites, unemployed. Income figures show the same marked difference. Using the income categories employed in Table 3-1, 39.6 percent of all whites in Oakland in 1960 were living in deprivation or poverty; 66.1 percent of all nonwhites were in these deprivation-or-worse categories.[6]

The Working Poor and the Average Worker
Until recently most poverty and welfare programs have generally ignored the plight of millions of working people who have employment, often full-time or with overtime, yet still have incomes in the deprivation category. In the United States over 200 occupations listed by the Department of Labor in 1968 paid less than $6,000 a year, and over 80 occupations paid under $3,800 annually. Some 30 occupations—including porters, laborers, and janitors—earn under $2,800, while a bootblack makes around $847 for an entire year.[7]

Above the working poor is the average-wage worker whose wages are too high for him to qualify for welfare and special Federal programs, but too low, for example, for him to move to a middle-class suburb. Father Paul Asciolla, editor of a Chicago newspaper for Italian-Americans, speaking at the United States Catholic Conference on Ethnic Americans, in Washington, D.C., in the summer of 1970, remarked that "Nobody has done anything for ethnics since Social Security. Yet here they are being blamed for white racism. . . . The ethnics are just the people whose own jobs are threatened."[8]

Not all the limited-income workers are ethnics; in the San Francisco-

Oakland SMSA the largest ethnic population is Anglo-Saxon. But the fact of very modest incomes for the working nonpoor is a fact with political significance. The median income for all families in the Oakland area in 1960 was $6,839; average hourly earnings in manufacturing within the San Francisco-Oakland SMSA stood at $2.79 in 1960 and $3.19 in 1964.[9] The latter figure yields an annual income of $7,018 on a 2,200 work week, a wage which was then not much above deprivation for a family of four. Given this relative scarcity of self-earned income, it could be argued that the average manufacturing worker has everything to gain from entering into alliance with poverty and black groups around a common program, including, for example, demands for an upgrading of the urban educational system, elimination of income taxes on incomes below $10,000, a cheap system of public transportation, and the municipal ownership of utilities. Indeed the wage level for manufacturing workers suggests one limitation on the poverty program of the 1960s: the Office of Economic Opportunity (OEO) was designed to help only the most destitute, and separated this bottom stratum off from potential allies among industrial workers. The ability to define the problem is a fundamental power over the policy process, and in the seventies the blue-collar class may well enforce a broader view of the problem.

PRIVATE DECISIONS AND THE JOB SUPPLY

What areas of decision by the private industrial sector, both employers and labor unions, have had the maximum effect on the supply and distribution of jobs in Oakland? Are there some invisible functionings of the economy which have decreased the job supply, or are there some rather visible decisions to which part of the shortage and distribution problem can be traced? The relatively slow growth rate of the region's economy is basically responsible for the present shortage of jobs. Additionally, certain specific decisions stand out with particular visibility: decisions by major corporations to locate, or not locate, within the city proper; the postwar policy of the Oakland Chamber of Commerce to deemphasize Oakland and promote instead the entire Eastbay region for new plants; decisions by local manufacturers to leave the city; and decisions by employers and unions to discriminate against nonwhites. How have each of these decision areas contributed to the city's present economic crisis?

Decisions by National Corporations to Locate or Not Locate in Oakland

Like any old city whose industrial boom came before or just after World War I, Oakland has failed to attract new industry. Its choice land sites are used up, it has a crime problem and a high level of unionization, and it has not attracted the aerospace or other growth industries of the postwar period. There is also considerable unwillingness among locally established businesses to let competitors do business in town. Hence partly because of its loss of attractiveness to profit-oriented corporations, partly because of its inability to capture growth industry, and partly because of local exclusionary attitudes, new industrial growth has taken place outside the old city.

The Decision to Deemphasize Oakland

Because of the loss of attractive industrial sites within the city, the Oakland Chamber of Commerce established, in 1935, its Metropolitan Oakland Area Program (MOA), intended to encourage the development of industry in the county, outside of the city proper. That local decision, coupled with the preference of national concerns for the green suburbs has substantially contributed to Oakland's decline. This program, instituted over 30 years ago, was beginning to be felt most severely in the 1960s, as South Alameda County absorbed an increasing amount of total investment in the County. In 1963, the MOAs Washington lobbyist—Vice Admiral Murray L. Royar, U.S.N., retired—helped the county get Federal money for the Alameda Creek Flood Control project to "help spur industrial development in that area." In part this "decision" was a recognition that the old central city no longer offered the possibilities for economic exploitation now offered by the suburbs, and that to insist on Oakland as the prime place for outside capital to invest would result in the loss of that investment. Since Oakland, like most small and medium cities, does not or cannot generate sufficient local investment to maintain a strong growth rate, outside investment in the city or county is an absolute necessity.

As a result of this new focus of energies, the decade 1952-1962 saw

Oakland, once the only major industrial center in the county, accounting for only 28 percent of all county industrial investment.[10] The war years intervened to stave off the logical consequences of the MOA program, but by 1960 the results of the program were plain. The city was, in that year, classified as a depressed area by the Federal government while within five years the city-located Chevrolet plant closed and a new General Motors superplant opened up only 30 miles away in suburban Fremont, creating a heavy swelling of population where jobs were not needed and depriving the old city of desperately needed jobs. In this process the county governments have been fully cooperative with the MOA program; the laws of the economy have not been directed by the laws of government, and city workers have paid the price. The regionalization of the city's economy has thus only aggravated the city's social crisis.

Runaway Industry

While new industry is staying out of town, old industry is getting out. The metal trades have lost over 3,600 jobs in the Bay Area since 1950, primarily because of plant relocations. Oakland has lost five big employers since 1960, and innumerable small ones. Cal Pak, whose Oakland employment fluctuated between 1,000 and 5,000 seasonally, has moved to the central valley. Most of the job loss due to move-outs is accounted for by the large firms. Marchant Calculators moved to Orangeburg County, South Carolina, where there will be no union, and where "the abundant reservoir of labor provides loyal, eager workers, willing to cooperate fully with management."[11] Marchant Calculators took 1,000 jobs with it when it left. Nordstrom Valve left Oakland for Texas and Nebraska, taking 1,200 jobs and a $5.7 million annual payroll. These plants were among the largest in the county. In one-half decade, between 1958 and 1963, Oakland's employment dropped by 3,200.[12] If Kaiser Industries left the city, as it could, 10,000 people would be out of work at a stroke, well over the 7,000 unemployed in the whole city in mid-1968. The possibility of leaving town gives employers a powerful trump in any dealings with city hall.

Race Discrimination and Jobs

Discrimination, like poverty, has its roots in the economic and social systems. All classes of industrialized society—ownership, working, and middle classes—have together been major agencies of discrimination against nonwhites in the United States. In the job market, discrimination is often attributed to racial prejudice among trade unionists, especially the craft unions; Nixon's Philadelphia Plan for integrating jobs in over 15 cities has been aimed primarily at the construction unions. Yet industry plays the major role in sanctioning job discrimination; rarely, if ever, have contractors or other construction company employers insisted that the unions they draw on for a labor supply should be integrated.

The result is widespread segregation in certain occupations, as is shown in Table 3-3. A similar pattern of underemployment obtains for Negro women. In each of 28 industries located in the Bay Area they comprised less than 2.5 percent of the work force.[13] Yet the 1960 census showed that blacks constituted 8.6 percent of the population in the San Francisco-Oakland SMSA.

Not all of these figures are the sole result of racial discrimination. Lack of experience or job training can operate as serious impediments

TABLE 3-3   Selected male occupations—number of employees and percent Negro, San Francisco-Oakland SMSA, 1960

Occupation	Number of employees	Percent Negro
Locomotive firemen	262	0.0
Power station operators	304	0.0
Spinners and weavers of textiles	24	0.0
Artists, art teachers	1,161	0.0
College presidents, professors, instructors	3,641	0.2
Engineers	17,992	0.3
Linemen, servicemen: telegraph telephone, and power	4,513	0.3
Accountants, auditors	10,485	0.5
Authors, editors, reporters	1,798	0.5
Dentists	1,832	0.6
Managers, officials, proprietors: salaried	43,006	0.6
Architects	1,184	0.7

TABLE 3-3 (Continued)

Occupation	Number of employees	Percent Negro
Pharmacists	1,526	0.7
Foremen: non-durable goods	3,499	0.7
Natural scientists	1,612	0.8
Salesmen, clerks	40,732	0.8
Tool and die makers	1,537	0.8
Brakemen, switchmen	1,101	0.8
Meatcutters	3,746	0.9
Farmers, farm managers	4,636	1.0
Designers, draftsmen	5,162	1.0
Managers, officials, proprietors (specified)	13,266	1.0
Teachers (elsewhere unclassified)	1,078	1.1
Foremen: durable goods	4,339	1.1
Bookkeepers	2,394	1.2
Lawyers, judges	4,164	1.3
All other professionals and technicians	20,282	1.3
Stationary engineers	4,540	1.3
Firemen, fire patrol	4,166	1.4
Physicians, surgeons	5,170	1.5
Officials and inspectors; state and local	2,318	1.5
Managers, officials, proprietors (self-employed)	27,321	1.5
Compositors, typesetters	3,361	1.7
Printing (excluding compositors, typesetters)	2,956	2.3
Fishermen, oystermen	241	1.7
Teachers: secondary	4,367	1.9
Cabinetmakers, patternmakers	1,697	1.9
Tailors, furriers	658	2.0
Blacksmiths, forgemen, hammermen	338	2.1
Social scientists	1,195	2.2
TOTAL	254,066	1.0

Source: William B. Woodson and Susan S. Sheffield, *Second Interim Report of the Oakland Adult Project Follow-Up Study,* Institute of Industrial Relations, University of California, for the Oakland Department of Human Resources, December, 1966, p. 116.

to minority employment, and employers are quick to point this out. Yet in many of the occupations listed above the amount of training required is negligible or easily obtained on the job. Meatcutters, brakemen, and clerks are in this category. Discrimination by unions is also a partial explanation of the figures, since many California unions have lower percentages of Negroes than the occupations listed in Table 3-3. The apprenticeship rolls, which display such a low percentage of Negro members, are decided upon, in California and other states, by joint labor-management committees, and management is in no way obligated by law to accept the apprenticeship program or the employees which come through it for hiring.[14] In the telephone industry, the company itself does the hiring, without any official union authority in this area, and until recently hired no Negroes for craft positions. Between 1964 and 1967, the state's leading privately owned gas and electric utility was found guilty of racial discrimination in employment practices nine times by the California State Fair Employment Practices Commission. During the same period a major airline and the state employment agency itself were also found to be discriminating by the commission (see Table 8-5).

Evidence of discrimination in Oakland has been published by local civil rights groups. A survey of 20 different Oakland restaurants, including the new Jack London Square establishments, was made by the Berkeley Congress of Racial Equality (CORE) in 1965. A total of 283 waiters and waitresses were observed, with the following result:

> Of the 283 waiters and waitresses observed, 245 were white, twenty-seven were Oriental and Mexican-American, and eleven were Negro. Of the eleven Negroes, four were in the back room at Sambo's for the sake of plantation atmosphere. The other seven were at Kwik-Way Shops, which is not properly speaking a restaurant. The other eighteen restaurants hired no Negroes at all as waiters or waitresses.
>
> Of sixty-seven bartenders, six were Orientals or Mexican-Americans and none were Negroes.
>
> Of eighty-five busboys, twenty-three were white, forty-five Oriental or Mexican-American, and seventeen Negro.
>
> Of fifty-nine cooks, six were Orientals or Mexican-American and nine were Negroes.[15]

Or in simpler terms, Negores were hired for out back jobs.

The CORE pamphlet containing this report stated that the President of the East Bay Restaurant Association had told CORE that the association did indeed have the policy of hiring only whites for up front jobs, but that the problem could be solved without conflict. In fact negotiations between CORE and the Association broke down. Several weeks of demonstrations, with as many as 200 imported demonstrators from the University of California at Berkeley, likewise failed to budge the association.

In the same year charges of hiring discrimination were made against the Oakland *Tribune* and its publisher, ex-Senator William F. Knowland. The Ad Hoc Committee to End Discrimination, a coalition which included the major civil rights and radical youth groups in Oakland and Berkeley, printed its own figures on the racial composition of *Tribune* employees. Ad Hoc's figures showed that the paper then had only 13 Negroes out of 1,255 employees. According to Ad Hoc's fact sheet 14 out of 18 administrative departments, including accounting, advertising, and mailroom, had no known Negro employees. The *Tribune* never denied those figures, but did, according to some employees, increase its hiring of Negroes just after the Ad Hoc demonstrations.

Thus the decisions by employers to hire whites instead of minorities

TABLE 3-4   *Enrollment in apprenticeship classes in Oakland, April, 1964*

Trade	Total apprentices	Total Negro
Steamfitters	88	0
Lathers	35	0
Electrical workers	117	1
Plumbers	63	1
Sheet metal workers	98	3
Painters	28	3
Roofers	27	4
Cement masons	46	5
Plasterers	38	7
Carpenters	119	25

Source: F. Ray Marshall and Vernon M. Briggs, Jr., *The Negro and Apprenticeship*, Baltimore: Johns Hopkins, 1967, p. 171.

gives particular shape to the unemployment pattern in the city. Discrimination among trade unions is another major source of decisions relating to minority nonemployment. In their book, *The Negro and Apprenticeship,* F. Ray Marshall and Vernon M. Briggs, Jr. present data on minorities in apprenticeship classes in Oakland in 1964. Their data are presented in Table 3-4.

Quasi-objective and subjective evidence of discrimination also exists in abundance in Oakland. Employers in California still use aptitude tests for employment.[16] Minorities and poor whites alike complain that any arrest record for any infraction of the law makes employment a near impossibility. Lack of high school diploma or the status of welfare recipient are also criticized as handicaps to employment. One local Negro, The Reverend John Burrell, went to work for the naval air station in Oakland's neighboring city, Alameda, in the early 1950s; by 1964 the whites who came to work in the same year had been advanced at least four steps, while Reverend Burrell had been promoted only one step above the lowest level, giving him a pay increase of only a few dollars a month. Reverend Burrell had a high school diploma and one year of college. After raising complaints with the U.S. Commission on Civil Rights, the Navy, and the local civil rights groups over conditions at the air station, he finally got some results: on December 15, 1965, the Navy fired him from his job.[17]

This brief examination of visible decision areas affecting the quantity and distribution of jobs has pinpointed some immediate areas that a democratic government would move into, to prevent the simmering racial crisis from exploding, and to reverse the city's growing trend of unemployment. But government activity so far has been totally ineffective. The unemployment figure has risen from 7,500 in 1968 to 15,000 in 1970, during the years that government has increased the number of its employment plans. Government should also step strongly into the question of discrimination in employment, if the present lopsided figures in many industries are to be reversed. Yet past experience suggests that strong government action will not occur; the Philadelphia Plan of President Nixon, an all-out governmental effort to open up jobs in Philadelphia, has raised black construction trade union membership from 1.01 percent to only 1.54 percent—just 35 new jobs, out of a total of more than 9,000 held by whites.[18]

THE REAL ESTATE INDUSTRY AS SUPPLIER:
HOW MANY HOUSES AND FOR WHOM?

The private housing industry has not been able, in this century, to supply enough housing for the nonaffluent classes. At the same time, cycles of the private construction industry have created severe housing shortages which were once periodic but are now a permanent feature of the city's economy. The first crisis shortage of housing occurred during the first period of rapid industrial development in the city, before and during the First World War. Early records of the city reveal the existence of a municipal Woodyard and Lodging House, a flophouse run by the city for the totally destitute and having a total of 180 beds; and a scattering of church-sponsored homes, totalling 150 beds. These constituted the charity aspect of housing in Oakland as of 1916, and reveal plainly that a housing shortage, related strictly to poverty, existed in the early days. In 1914 a professor of political science at the University of California, Berkeley, noted that "Oakland is full of unlovely tenement houses, vermin-infested lodging houses which produce crime . . . ." A report commissioned in 1916 by the chambers of commerce and city governments of Oakland and Berkeley stated that a substantial proportion of Oakland workers—those "unable to enforce a union wage"—was unable to afford new housing.[19] And union men who participated in the long and bitter strikes which have been the hallmark of Oakland's labor history were not uncommonly evicted from their homes before the organization of the CIO.

The Great Depression laid the basis for the present shortage. Its effects on the housing industry in Oakland were serious, and began the process of eliminating the small house builder from the market. The Oakland *Tribune Yearbook* for 1936 reported a drop in housing starts between 1926 and 1935 of around 300 percent. The result was a shortage approaching crisis proportions by 1938. Housing experts consider a vacancy rate below 5 percent to be a serious shortage. In Oakland the problem developed as shown in Table 3-5. Thus a blank spot in the development of Oakland's housing inventory helped lay the basis for the housing crisis of the war and postwar years.

Since 1938 the crisis has continued. Of the war years, the Oakland Housing Authority reported that:

To accommodate approximately 20,000 families that came to Oakland between 1940 and 1943, only 13,536 dwelling units have been
made available. Of these, 1806 were the reconversion of older
structures to multiple units. As a consequence . . . there has been a
housing shortage that has reached the proportions of a major crisis.
In April 1941, Oakland had a 2% vacancy rate. In April 1942, it was
.81%, and vacancies existed usually in higher brackets.[20]

Yet the political system, when it considered it necessary for the
successful functioning of industry, *was* able to increase the supply of
housing to workers and the poor. War workers flooding into the East
Bay area in the 1940s had no place to live. Accordingly the state of
California built minimal living accommodations for these industrial
workers, at no cost to local companies. Much of this housing was
supplied under the Federal Lanham Act, under which substantial housing was built nationwide for workers engaged in war production. Over
1,300 units of temporary housing was built for war workers in Oakland
under the act. Most, if not all, of the new units were built below local
building code specifications, as allowed by the act, to allow municipali-
ties to reduce costs of construction. The results were units barely
habitable. Some of the units, in multiple-unit structures simply called
dormitories, had neither cooking facilities anywhere inside the buildings, nor recreational facilities outside. Teenagers and all age groups
living in these barracks were almost wholly isolated from any social life;
the dormitories were located in and around the industrial sections of

TABLE 3-5   *Vacancy of rental dwelling units,*
            City of Oakland, 1931-1938

January 1, 1931	7.3%
March 1, 1932	8.5
March 1, 1933	6.7
October 1, 1934	7.8
May 1, 1935	7.4
March 1, 1936	4.5
March 1, 1937	2.6
March 1, 1938	2.3

Source: Adapted from Oakland Housing
Authority, *First Report,* 1938, p. 26.

the city. Work on permanent public housing in Oakland stopped in 1943, with the completion of 900-odd units which has been planned since 1938. The city made no new applications for public projects between December 1938 and April 1945. Thus Oakland built 400 more units for its wartime workers in those years than it built for its own poor, but the quality of the wartime housing was so low as to demean the lives of its residents.

In the early 1950s the City of Oakland surveyed local large employers, to see if their workers were experiencing housing shortages. Only one employer, the naval air station, reported any shortage, and this was not serious. The rule for governmental intervention in the housing supply in Oakland during and after the war seems to have been that action would be taken if it was required for the smooth operation of local productive enterprise, but not otherwise.

The post-World War II period was no different. The Federal Taft-Ellender Bill, which would have provided postwar public housing on a scale proportionate to the shortage, was defeated in the Congress in 1946. In Oakland, less than 400 units of public housing were built between 1946 and 1966, less than half the 1938-1943 total. In early 1946 the State Emergency Legislative Conference asked the legislature to appropriate $35 million for 70,000 emergency housing units in California. Governor Warren asked for, and got, $7.5 million to provide roughly 5,000 such units throughout the state.[21] This failure was due, in part, to the shortage of building materials immediately after the war. But the pattern of near-immobilization has characterized public housing programs to the present day. In Oakland, only around 1 percent of the city's 144,000 housing units are public housing.[22]

Nationally the picture is the same as in Oakland, as the director of the Department of Legislation of the AFL-CIO has recently made clear in testimony before a United States Senate subcommittee:

> ... in the thirty years since public housing became a federal program, only 650,000 public housing units have been built. Right now there are eleven million urban families whose incomes are low enough to qualify.

According to this same director, the present number of public housing starts in the country is 38,000, while to solve the housing shortage would require that the number of starts be increased to 300,000 starts per year in 1968 and 1969, and to 500,000 per year each year thereafter "until the crisis is overcome."[23]

At the same time that the public sector has been immobilized the private sector was laying the basis for crisis by failing to construct homes for low-income families. The director of research for the AFL-CIO stated before the same Senate subcommittee:

In the whole postwar period we put up very little low-income housing and also very little housing for the lower moderate-income families.

There has been a period of well over 40 years, nearly half a century, sir, in which there has been very little construction of housing to meet the needs of low income families and lower middle-income families.

Shortage conditions obtain nationally, as Table 3-6 shows.

In the summer of 1968 the problem was intensifying in Oakland, with local real estate officials predicting an increase in home prices of 25 percent by 1971. This prediction has come true, partially due to record high interest rates on home mortgages, so that owning a house is no longer ruled out only for the poor, but for many of the better-paid working-class and professional families. Thus we come to the decade of

TABLE 3-6   *Percent of white and nonwhite occupied units with 1.01 percent or more persons per room in selected metropolitan areas*

Area	White occupied units	Nonwhite occupied units
Cleveland	5.9	19.3
Dallas	9.3	28.8
Detroit	8.6	17.5
Kansas City	8.7	18.0
Los Angeles-Long Beach	8.0	17.4
New Orleans	12.0	36.1
Philadelphia	4.9	16.3
St. Louis	11.8	28.0
San Francisco-Oakland	6.0	19.7
Washington, D.C.	6.2	22.6

Source: U.S. President's Commission on Civil Disorders (Kerner Commission), *Report,* 1968, p. 258.

the 1970s with every expectation that increasing economic abundance will be accompanied by a continued shortage of housing for the poor and working classes.

Slumlords and Permissive Legislation

The clear consequence of this starvation of housing has been to force the nonaffluent into a housing market which is of low quality or into outright slums. The slum is the modern industrial solution to the housing needs of the poor, and Oakland is quite typical. But to explain the continuation of the slum housing supply we cannot look simply at the failures of the housing industry; we must look also at the functioning of government, without which slum properties could not continue. In Oakland, something over half the property in the far western, black area of town is absentee-owned income property; according to one city official, the Southern Pacific Railroad continues to be a major owner of property in the flatlands area between the freeway and the estuary, an area of intensive blight. The entire functioning of the housing industry is, at least potentially, subject to government regulation and direction; but in the area of slum housing the role of tax legislation is so clear that we note it here, anticipating somewhat the argument in Chapter Four about government policy.

According to Edgar Kaiser, President of Kaiser Industries, testifying as the Chairman of the U.S. President's Committee on Urban Housing before a Senate subcommittee in 1968, "Under existing tax laws, project owners may use these book losses to off set other income in computing annual taxes. . . . Accordingly many housing projects today are directly owned either by corporations or by individuals possessing other income. . . . The Internal Revenue Code allows partnerships to pass through such tax losses to the partners".[24]

Thus government tax policy becomes essential to the maintenance of the slum; the forces of the private market, as encouraged by government tax law, work daily to maintain and increase it. The failures of the private market are aggravated, not redressed, by public policy.

What areas of the private decision process by the real estate industry are markedly responsible for the present problems of the city? Again, as is the case of the manufacturing sector, we cannot here deal with a general economic theory of growth, and will simply look at those mechanisms and decision areas of maximum impact in creating the present crisis. We begin with the market mechanism itself.

The Market Mechanism: Will It Do the Job?

Inadequacy of the profit motive The private housing industry is in business, not simply to make houses, but primarily to make money. Maisel showed that the large builder in 1949 (making over 100 houses per year) received a 30 percent rate of return on investment, a very high rate.[25] On the dark side of this profit picture is the undisputed fact that there is simply no profit possible from building good housing for the poor. Government subsidy in some form is necessary as the industry itself realizes in the case of public housing.

Yet the high price of land, labor, and capital together, not just interest or profit on capital, suggest that subsidies to industry are no solution either. One housing industry journal put the problem succinctly:

New housing in multi-family buildings—the kind needed in city slums—costs from $17,000 to $22,000 a unit (in early 1968), even with an urban renewal land write-down. Rehabilitated housing costs at least as much, and sometimes more.

This means monthly rent for a $20,000 unit with one bedroom would be roughtly $150.00. That figure would include (1) maintenance, (2) operating costs, (3) amortization and interest on a subsidized loan with interest a few points below market yield and a term up to 40 years, (4) partial realty tax abatement (about 50%) and (5) a two-thirds write-down of the land cost. Yet half the low income families in the slums can afford to pay only $65 to $110 a month in rent, and the other half cannot pay over $35 to $60 a month.[26]

What this article implies is that even the most daring of the present housing programs, which call for massive Federal subsidies for private builders and big land and tax write-downs, cannot build a unit that the poor can afford. Hence we might conclude that one or both of two strategies are needed: a housing program where government itself acts as producer of the units, and massive upgrading of the purchasing power of the poor by eliminating economic cycles, high mortgage rates, and underemployment. But the whole history of the city's economy has shown the inability of the private economy as a whole to perform as the latter strategy requires, while the governments of nation and city are under pressure by private industry to stay out of the field of production, so that neither solution seems possible under the present system of American political economy.

The location of new housing: building units where they are needed least Like the city's manufacturing industries who have built plants in suburbs where jobs are not needed, the city's housing industry builds new housing units in areas of greatest affluence and least shortage. Of the total of 2,334 new single-family dwellings constructed in the city between 1960 and 1965, 1,716 of them, or over 73 percent, were constructed in only six census tracts which are among the lowest-density and highest-income tracts in the city.[27] The four most dense tracts in West Oakland reported a total of 10 new single-family houses constructed during the same period. New multiple-unit dwellings (apartments) constructed during this period show a more scattered distribution, but even here the concentration in investment has been around the expensive Lake Merritt area where rents reach as high as $300 per month. One new high-rise apartment charges an entry fee of $12,500 minimum, and $46,000 maximum, plus a monthly additional stipend. The six census tracts which border the Lake or are just to the north of it contain 4,099 new units, or 42.9 percent of the total multiple units constructed 1960-1965. All of West Oakland, the area of greatest deterioration, contains only 210 new multiple units, of which the majority lie just east of Market Street—close to downtown. Of the new residential construction built in the Bay Area between 1950 and 1960, 90 percent has been outside the city limits of Oakland and San Francisco where the most severe shortage exists.[28] Thus certain geographical areas, and the people living within them, have received the primary attention and benefit of the private housing industry. There is also a growing trend for the disparity in housing investment between different sectors of the city to grow larger. In West Oakland there has been for some years a building freeze, with practically no investment in new housing and very low rates of investment in housing repair. It is extremely difficult for the Negroes of West Oakland to get good financing terms for house repairs. As a result there is a tendency for this area to go into an accelerated economic decline due to capital starvation, while the Lake Merritt and hillside areas continue a normal rate of economic growth. This uneven development is largely a postwar phenomenon, and a major result of building houses for profit.

The Real Estate Industry as a Mechanism for Segregation

In this section we shall consider the decisions and policy of the real estate industry which have laid the basis for housing segregation in the city. We must begin by noting that descrimination and racism run deep in American society, and are not just confined to business and government groups. A study of Oakland in 1965 based on 328 interviews with local residents and businessmen concluded that three out of five Caucasians in Oakland ". . . harbor feelings of prejudice; the greatest degree against Negroes, the next against Spanish name persons, and the least against Orientals." The study also concluded that "one out of three Caucasians would act upon his prejudice in a discriminatory manner".[29] At the same time the study found discriminatory attitudes among representatives of the housing industry itself. From a total of 26 informants from realty and banking, 75 statements were recorded. Of these statements, 37, or nearly half, cited evidence of discriminatory practices related to keeping properties Caucasian-occupied. These practices included refusing to open listings to Negro brokers, block-busting, outright refusal to sell or rent to minorities, fast-talking or shaming a client out of the desire to buy or rent, raising the fear of being unwelcome, soliciting neighborhood opinions on race, charging higher interest rates, higher prices, and more discount points, and giving shorter loan terms. The report states that "it is correct to assume that out of a possible 670, at least 220 brokers and lenders in Oakland either practice or abet housing discrimination."[30]

The close relationships between banks and brokers makes discrimination possible.[31] One broker, well known in Oakland for the pro-integrationist views of his company, Central Realty, revealed an experience he had had with a large downtown bank. The bank at one time delayed making loans to anyone buying realty from Central Realty. Under pressure from his company the bank admitted that the reason for its action was that the Oakland real estate board threatened to withdraw all its accounts from the bank if the bank made loans for this company. In the opinion of this broker, the only reason the bank finally supported him was because his company was large enough to bring a good business to the bank. Because smaller brokers depend on the listings of large brokers, the latter can dominate the former. Thus if a large broker discriminates a small, dependent broker is almost required to do likewise. In addition, this broker's company had been denied membership by the Oakland Real Estate Board for over a year, in his opinion because of the integrationist policy of the company.[32] Membership on the board carries with it the right to place entries on the Multiple Listing Service, the central list of all homes for sale or rent in the city. Realtors who use this listing know that their entries are known by the vast bulk of realtors in the city, and they can have current data on the housing situation in the entire city as offered

TABLE 3-7   Total population, Negro population, Negro population as percent of total population, and median values of owner occupied houses, Oakland and suburbs, 1960

	Median value, owner occupied houses ($)	Total population	Negro population	Negro as percent of total population
Newark '	13,600	9,873	1	0.01
San Leandro	15,300	65,962	15	0.02
San Lorenzo	*	23,773	6	0.03
Union City	11,800	6,601	16	0.24
Orinda	27,700	4,712	13	0.27
Walnut Creek	19,000	9,844	31	0.35
Albany	14,400	14,894	75	0.50
Castro Valley	17,000	25,437	225	0.89
Piedmont	*	11,117	115	1.30
Alameda	14,900	63,855	3,127	4.89
Emeryville	10,400	2,675	473	17.69
Berkeley	16,600	111,268	21,850	19.64
Richmond	13,000	71,854	14,388	20.00
Oakland	14,200	367,548	83,618	22.75

Source: 1960 Census.
*Not available

by other realtors. Membership on the Multiple Listing Service comes only with membership in the Real Estate Board, and is obviously of great financial value to any individual company. Yet Central Realty sells houses to Negroes in white areas. For over a year, up to 1967, this company was refused membership on the board. Finally the company threatened a law suit; at this the board, with the greatest reluctance, admitted the company to its membership and placed its entries on the Multiple Listing Service. In Berkeley, Central Realty did take the local real estate board to court and won a court order that it be admitted to board membership.[33]

Racial discrimination by the housing industry in the suburbs surrounding Oakland is suggested by Table 3-7, which shows the very low percentage of Negroes living in most of the city's suburbs, including those where the average income would put housing within the price range of many blacks. Nearly half the Negro workers in Oakland in 1960 were skilled, professional, and clerical, earning $5,000 or more annually.[34] For these people a house in San Leandro, Albany, Union City, or Alameda is financially possible. But race discrimination in housing, as Table 3-7 suggests, keeps Oakland, Berkeley, Richmond, and Emeryville the locus of Negro concentration for the Eastbay area.

SOCIAL CONSEQUENCES OF PRIVATE DECISIONS

High Rents and Mortgages

An immediate consequence of the shortage of housing has been a high rent structure for the city generally, and especially the older buildings where the poor, white and nonwhite, are located. By now evidence that the poor pay more is a well accepted thesis[35] and Oakland is no exception. Average rents on older buildings in general have increased relatively faster than rents on new, post-1945 buildings, suggesting that rent gouging is not simply an isolated phenomenon (see Table 3-8). Rent for the elderly, whose age and lack of political representation makes them an easy target, and the conditions of housing for any given rent for the elderly is often very bad. The census for 1960 shows Oakland's population over 65 years of age approximated 45,000. It is estimated that in 1963 about one-half of this elderly population had a cash income of under $1,000 annually.[36] For those of the elderly who

TABLE 3-8 Rent increases in Alameda and Contra Costa counties, 1961-1966 (1960=100)

		Price range			Year built		
	Over-all	Under $17,500	$17,500-27,500	Over $27,500	Pre-1940	1941-1955	Since 1955
1961 Apr	101.4	101.5	101.1	102.8	101.2	101.8	101.4
Oct	102.9	102.9	102.8	104.4	102.8	103.4	102.2
1962 Apr	104.3	104.1	105.2	104.4	104.5	104.5	102.4
Oct	105.7	105.9	105.0	105.2	105.2	106.9	102.4
1963 Apr	108.9	109.6	106.7	106.3	108.3	110.9	103.2
Oct	110.8	111.4	107.9	108.5	110.8	111.8	104.2
1964 Apr	114.5	114.9	110.8	114.6	116.5	114.1	105.6
Oct	117.5	118.7	112.6	117.9	119.8	117.5	107.9
1965 Apr	119.7	121.3	114.5	119.9	122.9	119.5	109.4
Oct	122.5	124.8	117.1	121.9	126.2	122.0	111.7
1966 Apr	124.1	125.0	119.8	124.1	127.1	123.8	114.2
Oct	125.0	124.1	121.6	125.6	126.5	125.0	116.1

Source: Bay Area Council, *Northern California Real Estate Report*, Fourth Quarter 1966, p. 11.

have physical stamina and financial resources, private retirement homes or leisure world retreats offer a solution; but for the majority of Oakland's elderly the cost of such places is prohibitive.

Sheer physical strength is another problem. A recent urban rehabilitation program in East Oakland uncovered 33 cases of elderly people too feeble or unmotivated to care for themselves, yet living alone in squalor. The committee appointed to study this matter recommended the stark expedient of legal eviction if efforts at voluntary removal should fail. The city's Council of Social Planning estimates that over 25 percent of the population in the Chinatown redevelopment area have low enough incomes to qualify for public housing under requirements established by the Oakland Housing Authority. Up to one-quarter of the city's Mexican-American population qualifies for housing assistance, while for large families the problem of housing is almost insurmountable since landlords with low-rent units often refuse to take any large families regardless of race. Average rents in Oakland for a one bedroom apartment in 1968 ran between $90 and $125; yet the rent-paying ability of Oakland's poverty-class population in that year was between $40 and $80.

For many in Oakland, home ownership really means one or more mortgages. While exact figures for the city are not readily available, the

TABLE 3-9   Estimated number of all mortgages recorded and of junior mortgages recorded for property purchases and for nonpurchase purposes for Alameda County, 1953-1960

Year	Total no. of Alameda County mortgages	Total no. of junior mortgages	Junior mortgages as % of total
1953	24,480	8,940	36.5
1954	24,900	7,720	31.0
1955	31,360	8,200	26.1
1956	28,200	9,580	34.0
1957	23,980	9,430	39.2
1958	26,020	9,340	35.9
1959	28,360	11,120	39.2
1960	29,080	10,960	37.7

Source: A. H. Schaaf, *The Supply of Residential Mortgage Funds in the San Francisco Bay Area, 1950-1960,* University of California, Real Estate Research Program Report, no. 19, 1962, p. 55.

number of mortgages and junior (second) mortgages in two East Bay counties are given in Table 3-9.

It is not uncommon in West Oakland for homeowners to have a third mortgage, at flagrantly exhorbitant rates of interest, conditions which in themselves account, in large measure, for keeping the poor in poverty.

Segregation and High Rents

By limiting the areas open to black occupancy, the real estate industry is able to charge a higher level of rents to blacks than whites. In every city in the country a larger percent of blacks and non-whites pay over one-third of their income for rent than do whites; in Cleveland, only 8.6 percent of whites pay over one-third of family income for rent, while 33.8 percent of nonwhites do; in Los Angeles-Long Beach the figures are 23.4 percent for whites and 28.4 percent for nonwhites; in the San Francisco-Oakland area the figures are 21.2 percent for whites and 25.1 percent for nonwhites.[37] Thus it is obvious that blacks are paying, in general, a higher percent of income in rent. With the housing market segregated, confining nonwhites into certain areas makes it easy to charge high prices for units which could not bring such a price in the white areas.[38]

One would like to think that realtors are growing more enlightened. But when one realizes that segregation makes possible a higher, exploitative rate of rent, and that the private industry is a for-profit industry, then it seems that there are no corrective mechanisms within the industry which might lead it to a strong stand for integration.

A major consequence of housing segregation is segregation of the schools in Oakland, as indicated in Table 3-10. As the table shows, almost half of Oakland's elementary schools were 90 percent or more totally black or totally white in 1965. Carl Munck school, for example, named after a long-time school board member with high prestige among Oakland's civic groups, was 94 percent white—a symbol of segregation. Cole school was 98 percent black in that year; Hillcrest, 98 percent white. A more even distribution of races obtained in the city's high schools in the same year, with one exception: McClymond's High, 98 percent white and 0.6 percent Negro. An inequality in facilities was observable by an outside inspection of schools; flatlands and middle-income area schools had portable classrooms crowding lawns and playing fields, while the hill area schools had fewer or no portables.

Thus discrimination in housing leads to discrimination in schools. But it is also true that deliberate location of schools in districts guaranteeing a largely segregated student body perpetuates segregation in housing, and that the real estate industry itself is interested in seeing that school boards locate new schools in all-white areas to improve the saleability of real property to whites. The latest high school in Oakland, built in the mid-1960s, was located in a newly created north-south school district which contained only the white, $10,000 and above income families in the hill area. Had the new building been located closer to the center of town it would have had a racially diverse student body. CORE and the NAACP vigorously protested the site but to no avail; the school board designated the all white district and built the school. The kind of pluralistic decision process typical of American school politics resulted in a racist decision.

Finally, the greatest social consequence of this policy of discrimination and segregation is to create a growing hostility between the races. Racial violence is a very likely outcome. It is blamed on white racism or on troublemaking Negroes, depending on whether liberals or conservatives are speaking. Yet as the above should make clear, de facto segregation in the North is no accident; is the product of the housing industry's decision process and for-profit motivation. It is with that industrial level of decision process that the problem begins, and it is at that level that, ultimately, it must be solved.

TABLE 3-10   *Racial composition of Oakland's elementary schools, March, 1965*

Percent	Black	White	Total (black and white)
90-100	14	10	24
80-90	1	7	8
70-80	2	3	5
60-70	5	2	7
50-60	7	6	13
Total Schools:			57

Source: Oakland Public Schools, Office of the Superintendent, "Racial Composition of Student Bodies, November 1962-March 1965."

CONCLUSION: THE ECONOMY AND URBAN PROBLEMS

In the above pages we have considered the supply function of the city's manufacturing and housing industries; the areas of decision process with maximum consequence to the whole urban society, and what those consequences have been in terms of rent structures, segregation, joblessness, and school patterns. What has been shown is an enormous private area of decision making, the private economy itself. The generally sluggish rate of development of the national economy, and specific decisions made by local corporations, have been largely responsible for the existence of the city's poverty stratum of large dimensions, unable to find jobs and, consequently, quite unable to enter into the new housing market. Moreover the business "decision system", since it is almost entirely a for-profit system, realizes all of its present economic priorities by maintaining maximum freedom from governmental constraint. There is, in the entire apparatus of the corporate decision making structure, no inherent motive for integration, dispersion of wealth, or effective anti-poverty programs; there is considerable business motivation, on the other hand, to *oppose* programs of government intervention as supplier of jobs, housing, or income, either because such programs will cost the corporations more in tax money, or because they raise the specter of government competition with the private sector. As a result, the most that private industry will support in the way of economic reform measures are those relatively trivial measures which in no way threaten the functioning of the private firm. This basic self-interest accounts for local business nonpressure for significant economic reform; it accounts for the strong reaction of the Oakland business community against the possibility of a labor takeover of city government after 1946; and it underlies, as we shall see next, the performance of Oakland's city government in the areas of jobs and housing the years since 1945.

NOTES

1. Dividing the years 1948-1963 into periods of strong economic expansion, slow expansion, and no expansion, Burton Weisbrod has recently noted what happened to poverty levels during each group of years: "If the $3,000

family-income measure (of poverty) is used, the results show that in years of strong expansion, the number of poor families declined by an average of 667,000 per year; in the slow-expansion years the decline was a third less: 425,000 families per year; and in the no-expansion years of downturn or recession, the number of poor families *rose* by 400,000 per year. Thus the difference between strong expansion and recession has been more than a million families . . . among the poor". Burton Weisbrod, ed., *The Economics of Poverty, An American Paradox,* Englewood Cliffs, N.J.: Prentice-Hall, 1965, pp. 16-17.

2. Even the Lynds are more concerned with unemployment resulting from the depression than with poverty as a part of the economic system. See Helen and Robert Lynd, *Middletown in Transition,* New York: Harcourt, Brace, 1937, Chap. 2.

3. Thus Ricardo wrote: "Labour, like all other things which are purchased and sold, and which may be increased or diminished in quantity, has its natural and its market price. The natural price of labour is that price which is necessary to enable the labourers, one with another, to subsist and perpetuate their race, without either increase or diminution". In *The Works and Correspondence of David Ricardo,* ed. by Piero Sraffa, Cambridge, England: Cambridge, vol. 1, p. 93. Quoted in J. K. Galbraith, *The Affluent Society,* New York: Mentor Books, 1958, p. 33.

4. See esp. Paul Sweezy, *The Present as History,* New York: Monthly Review, 1953; Paul Baran, *The Political Economy of Growth,* 2d ed., New York: Monthly Review, 1968, and Baran and Sweezy, *Monopoly Capital,* New York: Monthly Review, 1968. An interesting discussion of recent Marxist and mainstream economic writings is in Robert Heilbroner, *Between Capitalism and Socialism*, New York, Vintage Books, 1970.

5. U.S. Department of Labor, "Subemployment in the Slums of Oakland," 1967.

6. The absolute number of poor and deprived whites is greater. In 1960 27,350 whites were below deprivation, compared to 19,030 nonwhites and persons with Spanish surnames, as reported by Gene Bernardi, "Characteristics of the Spanish Surname Population in the City of Oakland," *Oakland Interagency Project, 1965.*

7. U.S. Bureau of Labor Statistics, *Monthly Labor Review,* March 1965, pp. 249-255.

8. "Ethnic Workers Angered by Plight", *Milwaukee Journal,* June 17, 1970, p. 14.

9. Bank of America, Economic Research Department, *Economic Profiles of California Counties,* April, 1966 (no pagination).

10. Oakland Chamber of Commerce, Metropolitan Oakland Area, "Alameda County, California, Annual Report 1962," p. 2.

11. J. Ezekiel, "Marchant Moves South," San Francisco, California, Department of Employment, Coastal Area Office, 1965, p. 6.

12. *Census of Manufacturers, 1958, Census . . . 1963.*

13. William B. Woodson and Susan S. Sheffield, *Interim Report of the Oakland Adult Project Follow-Up Study,* Oakland, Department of Human Resources, June 1966, p. 117.

14. George Straus and Sidney Ingerman, "Public Policy and Discrimination in Apprenticeship," *The Hastings Law Journal,* 16, no. 3, February 1965, pp. 285-331, at pp. 311 and 315. A critique of the apprenticeship program can be found in Herbert Hill, "Racial Inequality in Employment: The Patterns of Discrimination," *The Annals of the American Academy of Political and Social Science,* 357, January 1965, pp. 30-47.

15. CORE, "The CORE Restaurant Project," Berkeley, April 21, 1965.

16. That aptitude tests are unnecessary and discriminate against nonwhites is asserted by many experts. Nixon's Chairman of the Federal Equal Employment Opportunity Commission, William H. Brown III, has promised "challenging of such screening devices as arrest record surveillance, English language skills, personal history and references, and heights and weight standards," Milwaukee Sentinel, May 22, 1970, p. 4.

17. (Oakland) *Flatlands,* February 10, 1967.

18. This fact, and the general picture of employment and public employment in American cities, can be found in Bennett Harrison, "National Manpower Policy and Public Service Employment," *New Generation,* Washington, D.C., Winter 1971, pp. 3-14.

19. Werner Hegemann, *Report to the City Council of Oakland, California,* 1916, p. 118.

20. Oakland Housing Authority, *Report,* 1944, p. 35.

21. California *Labor Herald,* March 29, 1946, p. 7.

22. Alameda County Council of Social Planning, "The Case for Additional Low-Income Public Housing in Oakland, California," July 21, 1966, p. 6.

23. Andrew Biemiller, statement in *Hearings by the Subcommittee on Housing and Urban Affairs, U.S. Senate Committee on Banking and Currency, Housing and Urban Redevelopment Legislation of 1968,* March 1968.

24. Edgar Kaiser, Ibid., P. 284.

25. Sherman Maisel, *Housebuilding in Transition,* Berkeley and Los Angeles: University of California, 1953, p. 132.

26. *House and Home,* special report "Business and the Urban Crisis," February 1968, p. C-10.

27. Figures complied from maps furnished by Oakland's "701 Housing Project," 1966.

28. Katherine Bauer Wurster, *Housing and the Future of Cities in the San Francisco Bay Area,* Institute of Governmental Studies, University of California, Berkeley, 1963, p. 5.

29. Floyd Hunter, *Housing Discrimination in Oakland, California,* Oakland, 1964.

30. Ibid., p. 41.

31. Robert B. Pitts, in the early 1960s Deputy Regional Administrator of the Housing and Home Finance Agency and former housing market analyst and

racial relations officer with the FHA, has written the following: "Racial discrimination in the real property market has long been supported by banks, savings and loan associations, and insurance companies, principally through their power to approve or deny loans. Although a few lending institutions are altering practices that foster discrimination, the majority continues to employ them." R. B. Pitts, "Mortgage Financing and Race," in John H. Denton, ed., *Race and Property*, Berkeley: Diablo Press, 1964, p. 99. This volume consists of the papers presented to a conference on race and property conducted by the University of California, Berkeley, Extension.

32. Interview with a Central Realty official, June 1965.

33. Slaughter v. Berkeley Board of Realtors. Case #334342, Superior Court of Alameda County, March 29, 1965.

34. Alameda County Council of Social Planning, "Population Trends in Alameda County," 1963, pp. 23-25.

35. David Caplovitz, *The Poor Pay More; Consumer Practices of Low Income Families*, New York: Free Press, 1963.

36. Alameda County Council of Social Planning, op. cit., p. 7.

37. U.S. President's Commission on Civil Disorders (Kerner Commission), *Report*, 1968, p. 289.

38. Among others, Chester Rapkin has made this point. See his "Price Discrimination Against Negroes in the Rental Housing Market," *Essays in Urban Land Economics*, Los Angeles: Real Estate Research Program, University of California, 1966. See also George Sternlieb, *The Tenement Landlord*, New Brunswick, N.J.: Rutgers, 1969; William K. Tabb, *The Political Economy of the Black Ghetto*, New York: Norton, 1970; and Robert Allen, *Black Awakening in Capitalist America*, New York: Doubleday, 1970.

PART

2

The Making
of Public Policies

CHAPTER FOUR

Private Industry and Public Housing Policies

In this chapter we will examine the extent to which the private housing industry and local business generally are able to direct the policies of city government in the area of housing.

NONINTERFERENCE AND DEMOLITION

The result of housing policies of Oakland and California agencies has been twofold: on the one hand, there is practically no government interference in the private housing market in the city. On the other, various government agencies have destroyed thousands of existing low-cost housing units and will destroy thousands more in coming years to make way for a variety of projects.

Government Noninterference in the Private Market

Housing in Oakland, despite over 25 years of Federal public programs, is almost entirely a private affair. Out of 144,000 units within the city, 1,422 units, or less than 1 percent, is public housing. The other 99 percent of the city's housing is privately built and owned. Federal intervention in this private preserve has been limited. Through the Federal National Mortgage Association (Fannie May) it has offered some low-interest real estate mortgage money to the city, but this has accounted for less than 10 percent of Oakland's mortgage money. FHA and Veterans Administration loans, which bring the possibility of greater Federal control over the private market, are also a very small fraction of total mortgage money in the Bay Area. The *Northern California Real Estate Report* shows that in 1964, out of a total of 9,275 mortgage loans made by all sources in the San Francisco-Oakland SMSA, only 334 were made by FHA or VA.[1] In short only about 3 percent of Bay Area loans came from the Federal government in 1964. With such a small share of the mortgage market the Federal government is in no position to dictate mortgage terms to the industry as a whole.

The Federal government is not the only level of government whose general approach has been to stay out of the private real estate industry. Local and state governments in California have likewise played only a minor role in the development of housing. When Governor Earl Warren created a commission on housing in 1947 the opposition from the private industry was so effective that the commission issued a four page report and resigned in a year for lack of funds. Between 1948 and 1961 no serious efforts were made at the statewide level to ease a housing crisis which grew, after the war, in all parts of the state. In 1961 the California legislature did create the Governor's Advisory Commission on Housing Problems (Eichler Commission). The commission was charged with studying the needs for housing of low- and middle-income households in California. In its report the commission stated that most of the 2 million new houses built in California in the decade previous to 1963 were bought by those in the top 30 percent of the income scale, and that over 700,000 housing units (over 13.5 percent of the state's total supply) were classified by the 1960 census as not sound or without all plumbing facilities. The report called for the creation of a state housing agency with broad authority to support housing construction "particularly for low-income families,"[2] a call which directly resulted in the proposal for a state housing and community development department in 1963. But the proposed agency lacked necessary tools. It had no program authority; it could not issue bonds or use the financial credit of the State of California to enter the field of low-cost housing, although this was a power recommended by the commission report. In short the proposed department was powerless to solve the housing needs of poor and middle-income families.

Even in this emasculated form the housing industry opposed it and defeated it entirely in the 1963 session of the legislature.[3]

The state has also failed to enter vigorously into the field of racial discrimination (see Chapter Three on discrimination and jobs). The 1963 Rumford Fair Housing Law, the most serious attack on the power of the private housing industry in recent years, has had only a limited effect. Administered by the California Fair Employment Practices Commission (FEPC) and stipulating a $500 fine for proved violators, the results of the act are shown in Table 4-1. Item one, Corrective action effected, refers to the number of cases where discrimination in housing was found by FEPC and something was done about it. This category averages about 120 cases a year. That discrimination is greater than this figure is suggested by the fact that Table 4-1's figures refer both to sale and rental of housing; there are literally tens of thousands of such transactions in California in a year. The suburbs are growing rapidly on an almost exclusively all-white basis. The FEPC, with a staff of only 50 persons for all of California, has jurisdiction over alleged cases of discrimination in the area of employment as well as of housing. To fight discrimination in jobs and housing with a staff of 50 in a state of over 18 million souls is a difficult job at best. Thus in the problem areas deriving from private industrial power, the general policy of government at all levels has been to allow private industry to set its own policy.

Within this basic laissez-faire approach there have been some limited governmental efforts to solve problems in Oakland. During World War II 2,728 units of temporary war housing were constructed in the city. After the war an additional 500 units were forced out of a reluctant

**TABLE 4-1 *FEPC disposition of housing cases in California,*
*9/20/63 through 12/31/66***

Corrective action effected	115
Insufficient or no evidence of discrimination	110
Public hearing held	1
No jurisdiction	28
Complaint withdrawn	61
Total	315

Source: FEPC, "Employment Case Statistics."

city council by and for returning veterans.[4] In addition the city has constructed, from 1945 to 1965, an additional 506 permanent public housing units in five different projects; and since 1966 has created leasing programs, rent supplement programs, and passed a bond issue for an additional 2,000 units of permanent public housing. But at the most these new programs will provide 4,000 units of new or subsidized housing for Oakland, in a city where over 24,000 families qualify for housing assistance.[5] The elderly population of the city numbers around 45,000 (over 65 years of age); half of this group, or around 22,500 earns under $1,000 total annual income per family and is in desperate need of some form of income supplements. Yet as of early 1966 Oakland was providing no rent subsidies, and its public housing project for senior citizens, Palo Vista Gardens, has only 100 units. Even the low rents charged by the Oakland Housing Authority are too high for substantial numbers of Oakland's poor. In 1946 the Authority estimated that 19 percent of Oakland's families were "of an income so low that even public housing cannot accommodate them."[6] Two years later the Authority estimated this number had risen to 20 percent. Today the Authority does not publish such statistics.

Laissez-faire also shows in the slowness with which the city has seized opportunities lying easily within its grasp. In 1950 the city received "from the (U.S.) Public Housing Administration. . . .a Program

TABLE 4-2   Destruction of housing units in Oakland, 1955-1965

Project	Units eliminated
Discontinuation of temporary public housing	1,382
U.S. post office site in West Oakland	312
Grove-Shafter Freeway	625
Bay Area Rapid Transit (BART)	450 (est.)
Acorn Redevelopment Project	1,790
Enforcement of housing code	2,250
MacArthur Freeway	500 (est.)
Total	7,309

Source: Oakland 701 Project, "Changes in the Housing Inventory in Oakland, California," 1966.

Reservation for 2,000 units of low-rent housing."[7] A program reservation is a promise from the Federal government to pay almost the full amount of the new units. Yet the work on this grant of public housing units has dragged. The average completion time for Oakland's first three public projects was under five years (1938-1943). The 1950 program reservation for Oakland is still unfulfilled today, 20 years after the initial grant. Only 506 units in five projects have been completed, or about 25 percent of the total possible in 17 years.[8] Oakland was granted no additional units under the 1954 housing act. Thus not only did the city fail to provide housing assistance to the thousands who have qualified to receive it, it failed even to provide that measure of housing aid which the Federal government had agreed to pay for. It would be fair to conclude that the city has not in the past 20 years made an all-out effort to solve the housing crisis in Oakland.

The Destruction of Cheap Housing

The most visible result of government activity in Oakland in the postwar years has been the *widescale destruction of large amounts of the existing units of low-rent housing.* Cheap housing units destroyed by government in Oakland far outnumbered new public units built in the last decade: over 7,000 units have been eliminated since 1955. The city itself has eliminated 1,774 units of temporary housing units constructed during the war and returned the land to industrial use. An additional 2,250 units have been closed through enforcement of the city's new housing code. Of this latter figure, 1,200 were Skid Row type units in rooming houses and hotels on lower Broadway. Closing them cleared the way for private commercial redevelopment, but the city provided no alternative place to live for the residents. Partly as a result of this action Oakland today has between 500 and 1,000 homeless persons who sleep in boxcars and public parks with literally no house whatsoever.[9] Table 4-2 shows which government projects have accounted for additional demolition and closures.

The majority of this housing loss was absorbed by the poverty areas of the city. Out of the total number of units eliminated, 6,609 were eliminated from the four areas designated poverty target areas by the Oakland Economic Development Council. It is noteworthy that many levels of government, from the city to the Federal level, have projects responsible for bulldozing the poor.

The published plans of various government agencies for projects in Oakland suggest that the city and other governments have continued to add to the dimensions of the crisis. Figures released by city offices show that an additional 1,668 units of housing were to be destroyed in the years 1965-1970, exclusive of units destroyed by redevelopment. This is shown in Table 4-3.

In almost all of the projects listed in Tables 4-2 and 4-3, corporate enterprises have been the most important source of nongovernmental policy-making initiative. Urban redevelopment and the code enforcement program were projects initiated at the request of OCCUR, the civic planning group, which included all the major downtown business organizations in its membership. The MacArthur Freeway was largely planned by the Alameda County Highway Advisory Committee, itself composed of city, county and state officials, and members of the Oakland Chamber of Commerce.[10] Bay Area Rapid Transit (BART) is also heavily supported by state and local businessmen. The biggest corporations in the state donated large amounts of money to the public campaign to get the voters to accept BART. The extent of corporate involvement is suggested by the amount of financing offered. Each of the firms appearing in Table 4-4 later became contractors in the $1 billion BART project.

All of these "civic" projects have resulted in substantial profits for contractors doing the work and have resulted in long-term upgrading in Oakland's business potential. At the same time, they have worked

TABLE 4-3   *Projected number of families displaced by non-redevelopment projects, by race, 1965-1970*

Projects	Number displaced	White	Nonwhite
Code enforcement	900	210	690
BART	363	57	306
Public housing (over income)	20	10	10
Street improvement	25	13	12
Grove-Shafter Freeway	360	–	–
Total	1,668		

Source: From material prepared by the Oakland Redevelopment Agency and Oakland Housing Authority.

hardships on owners and tenants. Each project has provided some compensation for property owners, but because government compensation is based on market value of property at the time of government purchase it is never the value received on the private market. BART has taken houses in West Oakland for under $7,500,[11] an amount about one-half that which the "compensated" owner will be required to pay for even the cheapest new house in the Bay Area. In addition relocation services for displaced residents have been minimal in most projects; the city's code enforcement program has offered no relocation assistance whatsoever, nor did BART in the first few years of its existence.[12]

Public Housing Supply: Control by Private Industry

At first glance public housing for the poor has a democratic appearance. Here, after all, the city is trying to do something for people in need, even if the efforts fall far short of the mark. And indeed the evidence suggests that public pressure has in fact been one major factor, first in creating the public housing program during the New Deal and in its implementation in Oakland. Between 1945 and 1953, the California *Labor Herald,* house organ of the Congress of Industrial Organizations (CIO) in California, presented numerous articles and analyses of the housing shortage within Oakland and on a state and national basis. In Oakland the Oakland Veterans Council was formed after the war for returning veterans who literally had no place to live. The Council was composed of representatives of 53 community organizations, including the AFL and the CIO in Alameda County. After much effort, and at least four rebuffs by the city council, the OVC and county labor

TABLE 4-4   Corporate contributions to BART bond issue campaign

Corporation	Amount ($)
Parsens-Bechtel-Tudor	22,500
Kaiser Industries	25,000
Westinghouse Air Brake Division	12,000
Standard Oil	10,000
Bethlehem Steel Corporation	12,000
Other corporations	121,218
Free Services (billboards, ads)	30,000 (min.)
Total	232,718

council succeeded in pushing the city council to establish a mayor's emergency committee on housing, a committee which ordered the construction of several hundred units of public housing exclusively for the use of veterans.[13] And in 1966, a thorough study of the need for low-cost housing by the League of Women Voters catalyzed passage of a bond issue which authorized an additional 2,000 units, the last public housing project authorized for the city. Thus public pressure has existed and played a role in the creation of government housing programs. And it has done so despite the opposition of business groups. Frank Crosby, Vice-President of the Oakland Real Estate Board, says simply that "It is the opinion of the Real Estate Board that public housing has the seeds of self-destruction in it. Housing is a personal thing in America, and ought to be kept private."[14]

At the same time the city's small amounts of public housing have not come as a result of giant popular pressures overwhelming a united and defiant business community. Rather the decisions to go into public housing in Oakland have resulted from either the active or reluctant approval of major portions of the business community. The first Oakland public project was preceded by a letter from the President of the Oakland Real Estate Board to the city planning commission which said in part that:

the rental that a large percentage of this group (the poor) could afford to pay was not commensurate with the cost of providing adequate housing and, therefore, private enterprise could not hope to engage in the activity of providing housing to this group.

The letter concluded:

Therefore . . . we recommend that your honorable body take such action as may be necessary to call to the attention of the City Council of the City of Oakland the necessity for the creation of a "Housing Authority. . ."[15]

Thus public housing came to Oakland with the official consent of the real estate board. Federal law itself guarantees that the private market will not be encroached on by public units.[16] The construction of over 7,200 temporary war housing units, the largest public project the city has ever undertaken, was done with the support of the Oakland-based corporations, stimulated simply by the shortage of housing for wartime workers, a shortage which was so great by 1943, that it was interfering with war production.[17] Thus for the vast bulk of both permanent and temporary public housing construction before 1950, a major section of the business community approved the public construction, including the real estate industry itself.

On the other hand, since the postwar years Oakland has *not* built public housing because of industrial opposition. In 1950 the Federal Housing Administration granted Oakland a program reservation of 2000 units.[18] To execute this grant the city council signed a cooperation agreement with the housing authority authorizing the latter to construct the 2,000 units. Yet only a little over 500 of these units were built by 1968. As the retired executive secretary of the housing authority Edward Horwinsky puts it, after the agreement was signed "there was such strong opposition from the apartment house owners association and the real estate board that we didn't get anywhere at all."[19] But by 1962 the situation had changed. Urban renewal had destroyed over 1,000 homes and could not continue without some public housing to absorb families displaced by future redevelopment demolition. To quote Horwinsky again, "The community was in favor of redevelopment as such; all the groups that opposed us in 1950 were for redevelopment, but they realized they had to have more public housing." As a result of this need the November 1966 bond issue authorizing an additional 2,000 units of public housing had the support of the Oakland *Tribune* and the nonopposition of groups usually strongly opposed to any increase in public housing. The chamber of commerce, usually an outspoken opponent of any public housing which does not directly benefit Oakland's corporations, remained neutral. Opposition came from the real estate board, the taxpayers association, the Associated Homebuilders of the Greater Eastbay, and the apartment house owners association. Yet, according to Horwinsky, "The opposition of these groups was mild. Had they come out strongly against it, it would have made a difference." As it was the bond issue barely squeaked by with a margin of less than 500 votes, a margin which, in the estimate of those on both sides of the issue, would have gone the other way without the unusual editorial support of the *Tribune*.

Thus Oakland was denied almost 1,500 units of authorized public housing for 15 years because of real estate opposition, and now has an authorized 2,000 unit increase because the backers of urban renewal need public housing to make redevelopment a success. Negro or

Mexican-American political groups were too fragmented to initiate or force passage of the bond issue. The League of Women Voters, joined by the council of social planning and with the important political support of a liberal state assemblyman, Nicholas Petris, acted as the active force promoting the additional public units in 1966.

Public Housing: Who Benefits?

The above comments suggest that business groups have been primary beneficiaries of the public housing projects in several ways. The law guarantees that the public supply will not compete with any portion of the private market. Additionally, an early hope for public housing projects was that they would improve the market value of surrounding properties.[20]   Finally, the public projects in Oakland since 1943 have not resulted in the tearing down of any slums in Oakland since completion of the first program in 1943, although such demolition is called for in the cooperation agreement between the city council and the housing authority passed by the council in 1950 and reaffirmed in 1962. [21] Hence no slum owners have suffered from public projects. Also, public housing bonds are quite attractive to investors. They are tax-exempt and, in Oakland as of December 1966, were yielding a 4 percent rate of interest. The Bank of America, whose representative sat on the first housing authority in 1938, now buys all the authority bonds. Thus public housing on the mini-scale which private business permits has been good business for banks and no serious threat to private real estate interests.

Finally, the building trade unions and local government itself benefit financially from the projects. Unions benefit from construction contracts. The city and county have collected over $2 million of in-lieu tax payments from the public housing authority over the last 30 years.[22] The operating profit on rents received from these buildings over the same period of time constituted almost $3 million.[23] The city and the county have profited over $5.5 million in 25 years of public projects, a very large sum. And because the poor in the projects have been paying in-lieu taxes through increased rent, taxes on private property owners have been kept down to present levels. Indeed the tax returns paid from the rent checks of the poor in public projects could well be above the returns on the same property in private hands, since private property owners, especially large ones, have ways of appealing tax rates or avoiding them altogether. But the housing authority collects taxes automatically with the rent, like dues check-off for a union, while project residents on the whole are generally not aware that they, too, are taxpayers.

Public housing also offers a slice of the pie to the poor, as it does to banks, the construction industry, and local and county government. (The Oakland Housing Authority also pays an annual dues of $50 to the Oakland Chamber of Commerce.) But the difference is that for the poor, housing by public funds is needed as a solution to a problem, not as a small token. For the masses of the poor in Oakland, the over 24,000 families in need of public assistance in housing and qualified for it, the public housing program is wholly inadequate. A serious program to provide housing for the poor in Oakland would cost, as estimated in a report commissioned by the city government, $123 million.[24] Those are the dimensions of the problem. In the light of that fact the present program in Oakland can be seen as giving the appearance, but not the reality, of trying to solve problems.

GOVERNMENT POLICY AND NONWHITES

As in the preceding section on housing supply, government policy in Oakland in the area of discrimination fails to attack discrimination in the housing industry and thereby uses public policy to buttress private interests. In Oakland there has been no attempt by city agencies to limit private discrimination. Thus the city contributes to discrimination by its own acts of omission, or "non-decisions."[25]

The practice of illegal subdivision of apartments in Oakland during the war and the city's blinking at these illegal units since 1945 have been important factors in keeping Oakland segregated. In addition the practices of the real estate board in discriminating in listings, as well as discrimination by private lending institutions, went officially unnoticed by the city until November 1961. In that month, pressured by discontent among Oakland's Negroes, the Mayor of Oakland, John Houlihan, appointed the Committee on Full Opportunity (COFO) to investigate discrimination in housing. COFO took four years to produce its study of discrimination in housing in Oakland, although the actual report (the Floyd Hunter report)[26] was written by a consultant who completed the work within a year of being hired. The report, which found widespread evidence of discriminatory attitudes in the city's real estate industry, was submitted to the mayor on September 17, 1964. In June of 1965, COFO issued its own final report, based on the consultant's report, saying in part: "We have reached the conclusion that discrimination does exist and that it is a problem of such magnitude that it requires community commitment and mobilization for its obliteration."[27] The report went on to recommend the creation of a new action committee to combat racial discrimination and to work in the general area of providing "decent, safe, sanitary housing for all." The report left no doubt that it had found discrimination, and that it expected action: "Oakland should wage a systematic, continuous combat against community ignorance and resulting prejudice."[28]

This report by COFO was the first strong statement by any official Oakland agency on housing discrimination. The mayor, however, played the report down. The Hunter report which preceded COFO's final report received no publicity and practically no comment from the mayor's office. The final report of COFO also passed without official mayoral comment. By December 1965 one member had resigned. Finally on January 5, over a year after completion of the Hunter report and seven months after COFO's demand for a new action committee, the mayor replied. He charged that the work of COFO was only partly done, that the committee had failed to shine "the white light of publicity" on the all-white suburbs that create a wall around Oakland.[29] COFO rejected the mayor's criticism, and on February 18, 1966, Houlihan dissolved the committee. It had spent almost four years, made a thorough study of discrimination in housing in Oakland, and had not budged city hall an inch. No city committee on the subject has been convened since, and discrimination in Oakland's housing today is as prevalent as it was in 1950.

The city further aids discrimination by its positive activities as well as by its failure to act. Oakland's property-owning groups believe that the city is under attack from the influx of poor people, especially Negroes, and that if "those people" are not kept out of the downtown section and residential areas, the city will no longer be a place where they can do business or live. Consequently a number of things have been done by public agencies in Oakland which have resulted in keeping

poor people and Negroes out of certain areas of town. Housing discrimination, abetted by nonopposition from the mayor or city council is
one major element. Another has been the location of major projects.
Two thruways now divide Oakland; the first, the Bayshore-Nimitz, runs
along the boundary of the black-white division in West and East
Oakland. A new set of state buildings have cropped up where once
there were slums and declining small businesses along lower Broadway,
at the same time that the surrounding area was being developed for
semiluxury restaurants and nightclubs. Operation Padlock resulted in
closing, for building code violations, the remaining old hotels along
Broadway near downtown at the edge of the black district. As a result
the whole of Broadway is becoming a wall of public buildings, private
business offices, or high-priced restaurants and stores with no places for
the poor to eat or sleep—a barrier between the poor and downtown.
The city's police department stands in a $14 million building on lower
Broadway, put there, in the words of one long-time observer, to
"anchor lower Broadway."

Part of the city's policy of "containment"[30] can be seen in the
choice of sites for the city's public housing projects. The first two
permanent projects were located, during the Second World War, in deep
West Oakland which by then was already predominantly black and
industrial. One other project was located at 1327 65th Avenue in East
Oakland, an address remote from downtown, in a poor section of town
on the periphery of the industrial section which rims the city. In
addition the 10 "temporary" housing projects built to house war
workers became almost totally segregated.

Of the permanent public housing projects, four were totally segregated—three totally white, one totally nonwhite—by 1950. Three other
projects had a total of 21 whites and 607 nonwhites. The remaining
two projects had ratios of 15 white to 529 nonwhite, and 475 white to
9 nonwhite.[31] In short, near-total segregation in housing patterns has
been the norm in Oakland, a norm typical of public housing in all
northern cities.

Thus while real estate board practices have kept Negroes out of the
middle-class hill area, the city government public housing projects have
kept them in deep West Oakland and close to the estuary. The fact that
blacks have spread over a steadily increasing area of the city since 1945,
despite city and private efforts at control, is due to the pressure of

sheer physical numbers of immigrants, and to the existence of a small but active black real estate industry.

LOCAL REGULATION OF THE PRIVATE HOUSING INDUSTRY

Rent Control

During the Second World War Oakland, like all United States cities, was subject to rent control laws both for private housing and commercial hotels. New York City still had selective housing price control in early 1971, left over from the Second World War. However, by June 1971, legislation was introduced in the state legislature of New York to decontrol *all* remaining housing units. In the postwar years and as late as January of 1952, a barrage of public attacks were mounted on President Harry S. Truman by major newspapers to drop all price control measures, including rent control. Prior to July, 1947, when selective rent decontrol entered into effect, a total of 15,700,000 housing units had been under Federal rent control. By September 1, 1952, the rent stabilization program was to come to an end for all apartments and houses "except in those areas where the local governing bodies by resolution, or the electorate by referendum, voted to continue rent controls after the date."[32]

The 1947 Act decontrolled rents for commercial hotels, and in Oakland the major downtown hotel increased its rates from 100 to 150 percent in some of its rooms.[33] Yet rent control of housing and apartment units remained in effect in the city, due to the intervention of Federal power: asked repeatedly by the local apartment house owners' association for a hearing to decontrol apartment rents, the local Federal rent board simply refused to hold hearings.[34] Requests by Oakland landlords for rent increases before the board, requests which usually were not granted, showed the amount of expected increases: rent in effect (as of 1950) $55, landlord requested $125; rent in effect $55, requested $148; $48 in effect, requested $130; $70 in effect, requested $150. No landlord was asking for less than $90 total monthly rental.[35]

In August of 1951 the city council held a public hearing on rent control. Only two groups present at the hearing favored the elimination of rent control over private rental property—the apartment house owners association and the Oakland Real Estate Board. Against the measure were speakers from the International Longshoremen and Warehousemen's Union, the Alameda County Veterans Association, the Alameda County CIO, the (AFL) Central Labor Council of Alameda County, the Boilermakers' Union, and dozens of individuals without organizational affiliation. Citing the housing vacancy survey which had been commissioned by the Oakland City Council during June and July, Robert Thorpe, director of the Alameda County Defense Rental Area, stated flatly at the hearing that his survey showed an over-all vacancy rate of 2.024 percent for all types of rental housing, and that there was a shortage of housing in both low and medium rental ranges.[36] The apartment house owners' association disputed this finding, using moral arguments and citing personal knowledge of the local market, although they had no figures with which to answer Thorpe. They also argued that rents could be expected to remain stable even without control, and argued that it was unfair for landlords to suffer the effects of control when most other commodities in the economy had been decontrolled. Speakers for rent control cited Thorpe's figures and pointed to the fact that decontrol in Los Angeles, which had had a 4 percent over-all vacancy rate at the time of decontrol, had resulted in rent increases of 40 percent in that city. However the city council agreed with the real estate groups, and on September 13, 1951 passed on a vote of eight to one a resolution stating that "there no longer exists such a shortage in rental housing accommodations as to require rent control in the City of Oakland."[37]

Thus in a dispute in which the interests of hotel owners and landlords were pitted sharply against the interests of roomers and renters of low or middle income, the city sided with the real estate interests. It is this decision made 20 years ago by the city council which accounts, in part, for the fact that in 1966 16,100 families in Oakland were paying over 35 percent of their income in rent, while over 29,000 families were paying over 25 percent.[38]

Building Codes and the Code Inspection Program

Building and related codes are a basic area of governmental housing policy within the jurisdiction of any municipality. What these codes say and do are of importance to the whole community, both from the point of view of safety, and from the standpoint of their impact on property values and living conditions of millions of people. This section considers who has written these codes in Oakland, how effective the building code has been in arresting blight, and who these programs benefit.

Oakland has five codes related to housing: the building, plumbing, heating and ventillating, housing, and sign codes. The general political process whereby these codes have been legislated in Oakland has been for the city and the affected industry to work out a code acceptable to both parties. The building code provides an example of this. The building code sets up standards for materials and construction methods, and specifies the size and location of buildings on lots. It is the creation of the International Conference of Building Officials. This conference writes the uniform statewide code on which local codes, including Oakland's, are based. The Conference has three types of memberships: building officials from state and municipal government; professional memberships, including architects and engineers; and industry memberships, primarily the producers of building materials. Thus professional and industrial groups are two-thirds of the membership types. Industry members can make motions on the floor and "do everything except vote."[39] The information on which code changes are based comes from industry as well as government members; proposals for code changes come from all members, including industrial and professional. In the code reform committee of the Conference "no one is cut off." Thus the code which is supposed to regulate the construction and safety standards of the housing industry is itself highly influenced by the industry to be regulated.

The major role of private industry is also shown in the method of adoption of the building code in Oakland. The 1946 building code adopted for California by the statewide Conference was adopted by Oakland in 1948 because, in the words of one Oakland building official, the code "has the background of thinking of industry, architects and engineers, and building officials."[40] Just how much of industry's thinking was included in the 1948 Oakland code is suggested by the process whereby Oakland adopted the new ordinance. For several weeks the code was "in the hands of a special committee of Oakland's Chamber of Commerce," a special committee chosen by the chairman of the chamber's Construction Industries Committee. This special committee held innumerable meetings on the proposed building code between the summer of 1946 and passage of the code in the summer of 1948 and gave the proposed code "a final check before sending it back to the city council for action."[41] The official mayor's committee which determined the city's policy on the code also included chamber members, including the then-chairman of the chamber's Construction Industries Committee.

The same major role was played by the chamber when Oakland adopted the uniform code of the Western Plumbing Officials Conference in 1949.[42] A subcommittee of the chamber's Construction Industries Committee actually prepared the heating and ventillating code which the Oakland City Council passed in 1950.[43] This subcommittee included, in addition to Dr. S. F. Farnsworth, Director of the Oakland Health Department, and Bill Ward, the city's chief plumbing inspector, a total of 13 businessmen, including the owners of two plumbing companies, two general contractors, and an executive of the General Air Conditioning and Heating Company. Many, if not most, of this subcommittee's members represented business firms which would be subject to regulation by the new code. Nearly every major supplier of gas and ventillating equipment in Oakland sat on the subcommittee. The board of appeals provided by the code to determine the acceptability of alternative materials and types of construction in heating and ventillating was also created by the chamber subcommittee. Thus industry itself wanted the appeals board to which violations and interpretations of the code can be appealed.

The scope of industrial control is also shown in Oakland's housing code adoption and enforcement. By the mid-1950s deterioration in Oakland's center city had grown so severe that a program of rehabilitation and renewal was begun. The major force behind this movement to save the city was the Oakland Citizens Committee for Urban Renewal (OCCUR), which included in its membership every large bank in the city, the only gas and electric company, the major downtown property owners' association, the real estate board, members of the chamber, and some government officials. The committee had the support of the Oakland *Tribune,* and was spearheaded in its early days by an executive of Kaiser Industries. In short most of the financial, and much of the industrial muscle of Oakland served on OCCUR. (For the role of this group in urban renewal and that of the whole program, see Chapter

Five, pp. 111 ff.) Under constant pressure from this wealthy and self-appointed committee the Oakland City Council was moved to change its housing policies. It is important to remember that the biggest change in Oakland's code enforcement policy since the Second World War was the result of pressure initiated by the economic giants who gave time and money to OCCUR.

The changes which were adopted by the city, and those which failed of adoption, illustrate the ability of the real estate and housing interests to influence local politics. Besides passing urban renewal measures, the city responded to the deterioration of its housing stock by passing the new housing code mentioned earlier and creating a housing advisory and appeals board to hear cases of presumed violation of the code. While the city passed its own building code in 1948, Oakland had no housing code of its own prior to 1958. Instead, the city relied on the state housing law, a document which was long on standards but short on enforcement sanctions. Few landlords went to court in Oakland under the state code. As one city housing official puts it, "The state law required that some enforcement be done, but it rarely was done."[44] In 1957 OCCUR adopted a resolution calling for the creation of the housing advisory and appeals board, to hear appeals from property owners charged with code violations. The resolution was adopted by OCCUR following working committee meetings attended by the important real estate organizations in the city, the construction industries department of the chamber of commerce, the Associated Homebuilders of the Greater Eastbay, and the Alameda County Building Trades Council. The resolution also called for the centralizing of all permit, license, and inspection services in one department of building and safety.[45] Such a department, in OCCUR's judgement, would have strengthened the power of the city to control building and housing code violations. The city council refused to create such a department. But it did create the housing advisory and appeals board, and adopted the proposed housing code.

The Oakland Real Estate Board (OREB) worked, in this case, through its Housing Code Committee, comprised of members of the Board itself, the apartment house association, and the East-bay American Institute of Architects, who provided some opposition to the code. After the code had been passed by the city council this committee recommended deleting two sections which included the only real enforcement mechanism. The code as originally passed in the fall of 1957 provided, in section 107.1, that "it is unlawful to either occupy or rent to another any residential building . . . for which a Certificate of Occupancy or Temporary Certificate has not been issued." A certificate of occupancy would be issued after a city inspector found that the building complied with the local building code. Only then could a building be sold. The Housing Code Committee of OREB objected to this section. In fact over 15,000 apartment buildings with illegal conversions, the result of the crisis shortage of housing during the Second World War, still existed in the city and could not be legally sold under section 107.1. As a result of this objection the city council scheduled a special meeting for September 10, 1957. Because certain members of the OREB could not attend on that date the council rescheduled the special meeting for October 24, 1957. On September 17, 1957 the council passed the new housing code ordinance, with verbal protest against section 107.1 registered by spokesmen for OREB.[46] The council was advised by the city attorney at that meeting that under state law final passage of the ordinance did not of itself put the new housing code into effect. The next day Fred Squires, director of the urban renewal section of the city department of building and housing, sent a letter to the council relating what happened immediately after the council action of September 17:

> The Mayor and some members of the Council talked with OCCUR, on the subject of certificates of occupancy. . . It was . . . indicated that it was the intent of the Council to exclude all family dwellings not solely owner-occupied from the "prior to sale" provisions [of the code.][47]

Since less than half of Oakland's housing is solely owner-occupied, the intentions of the council, as suggested by this memo, were obviously limited. The fact that the mayor and councilmen went to confer with OCCUR after the September 17 council meeting is a fact worthy of note.

The businessmen won the day a little over a month later. On October 24, 1957, the council repealed the two sections which the real estate board's Housing Code Committee had found offensive, and substituted the following amendment: "All residential buildings shall be deemed to hold an interim certificate of occupancy."[48]

The code now requires the seller to obtain a history of the conditions of the building and inform the buyer of this document, making clear any and all code violations. Realtors themselves benefit from this requirement, since they are among the greatest buyers of rental housing in Oakland. The new ordinance thus acts to protect the buying public and the industry itself from its less scrupulous members. Yet the new code offers no protection to the slum dwellers. Thus did the city council, on request, pull the teeth out of its new law.

The reform in housing has not been entirely without effect, despite the deletion of section 107.1. In 1959, the first year of the new code enforcement program, over 30,000 violations were corrected out of 50,000 reported violations. Each year since then approximately the same number of corrections has been made. Between 1961 and 1966, 1,252 substandard structures have been demolished in the city, due to the enforcement of the new code. After the first urban renewal project in Clinton Parks (for a description of the Clinton Parks project, see Chapter Five), the housing division in Oakland divided the city into 16 separate districts and began comprehensive housing surveys in each district for code violations.

Yet, despite this limited program, Oakland's physical stock of housing has continued to deteriorate. The inspection program has concentrated on visible hazards only, not full inspections with measurements of interior dimensions, checking of wiring plans, etc. From sixteen districts in 1959, the inspection program dropped to six districts by 1965, each with 1,100 units of housing. In the words of one official, "We're just holding the line." This same official estimates that, with present staff, it would take the housing division between 10 and 15 years to do all the survey and compliance work for the entire city.[49] And even this total job wouldn't eliminate existing safety hazards in Oakland. In a report to the city council and the mayor on January 7, 1958, then City Manager Wayne Thompson noted that "no amount of personnel or inspection frequency could ever eliminate more than a substantial percentage of the typical hazards with which these accidents [injury by fire] are most usually associated."[50]

The city, then, knows that safety hazards exist and pleads that inspection is incapable of solving the problem. But no one has offered any alternative suggestion, and in the meantime a price is being payed. On February 14, 1966 the Oakland *Tribune* reported the death of three black children in a fire which started from rags stuffed in a heater vent. First Assistant Fire Chief Robert Costa theorized that the rags "had been placed in the vent to keep out cold air." The article concludes: "Chief Costa estimated damage at $6,000." The mother of two of the dead children collapsed at the scene.[51]

PROPERTY TAXES AND THE LOCAL HOMEOWNER

Property taxation can be considered as a government policy toward homeowners and other property owners. Here we consider the bases of property taxation in the city and ask whether business and large property owners have obtained tax advantages over the small home-owner.

The Regressive Nature of the Property Tax

The property tax in California pays for the bulk of the expenses of city and county government, special districts, and school districts. It is the major tax source. In 1962 more tax money was collected through local property taxes than the State of California collected in state taxes: $2,433,000,000 in local property taxes and $2,314,600,000 in state tax revenues.[52] The property tax, as a tax source, far exceeds the yield to the state from sales and use taxes, which together provide 30 percent of the total state tax yield and are the largest single source of state revenue.[53]

The size of property taxes is important because the structure of these taxes is sharply regressive, meaning that the greatest single source of tax income in the state requires people of low income to pay a disproportionately high rate. This conclusion has been reached by all the recognized studies of California and other states, of which the best known is the study by Richard Musgrave for a congressional subcommittee on tax policy in 1955.[54] While data for Oakland and Alameda County are not readily available, a study by a professor at Pomona College gives the data for Los Angeles which characterize the statewide and national picture. As Table 4-5 shows, the current property tax laws hit the low-income people the hardest. Moreover, protests against the county's assessment rates, lodged at the Alameda County Board of Supervisors, seem to be made primarily by large property owners, and not the small ones. The *average* reduction in assessment for each protest in Alameda County between 1959 and 1963 was $7,522, a sum equal to more than half the total value of most houses in Oakland.[55] This suggests that the big owners were the primary beneficiaries of protest. Over the same four-year period the cummulative benefits were quite substantial: original tax bills were reduced by a total of $2,151,375.00 as a result of taxpayer complaints.

Corporate Influence over Tax Levies

Another way of looking at the property tax is to break it down by type of property. The constitution of the State of California requires that all property be assessed at 100 percent of its sale value, the amount the property would bring on the open market.[56] In fact this requirement has been disregarded for decades. Property of all sorts is assessed in California at a fraction of its full sale value. In Alameda County the

TABLE 4-5   Relation of household income to property tax,
Los Angeles County, 1959

Annual household income ($)	Property tax payment as % of household income
3,000	6.95
4,000	6.00
5,000	5.35
6,000	4.70
7,000	4.15
8,000	3.95
9,000	3.80
10,000	3.60
11,000	3.10
12,000	3.20
13,000	3.26
14,000	3.10
15,000	3.03
16,000	2.90
17,000	2.86

Source: Testimony of Gerhard N. Rostvold, Ph.D., of Pomona college, in Hearings before the Assembly Interim Committee on Revenue and Taxation, 1964.

percentages are as shown in Table 4-6. These ratios are in flux. Just after World War II both residential and business property (of all types) were each assessed at a higher rate. They have been approaching equality at least since 1947, as is shown in Table 4-7.

What Table 4-7 shows is a steady drop in the percentage rates of taxation in business and a much slower drop, culminating in a rise, in tax rates on residential property. Clearly since 1947 the official rate of taxation on business, commercial, and industrial property has been dropping much more rapidly than the rate of taxation on residential property. This has meant a windfall for business and only a slight gain for residences. The political process whereby this change has come about is explained, as regards the tax on business inventory (which will also drop by 1971) by Edouard B. McKnight, Secretary of the big-business supported Alameda County Taxpayers' Association:

TABLE 4-6   *Assessment ratios in Alameda County, 1966*

Type of property	Rate of property tax
Residences and apartments	21.6% of assessor's opinion of market value
Business, commercial, and industrial	28.0% of assessor's opinion of market value

Source: (Alameda County Taxpayers' Association) *News Facts,* March 16, 1966.

TABLE 4-7   *Alameda County tax rates on residential and business property, as a percentage of assessor's opinion of cash value, 1947-1971.*

Year	Residential	Business, commercial, industrial
1947	29.77	40.75
1955	*	36.00
1966	21.60	28.00
1971	25.0	25.0

Source: The figures for 1947 refer simply to Oakland, and not, as do the rest of the figures, to Alameda County as a whole. These 1947 figures come from the May 9, 1947 issue of *The Citizen,* the campaign organ of the conservative faction for city council election. 1955 and 1956 figures from *News Facts,* March 16, 1966. State law now requires equalization of residential and business rates by the year 1971.
*Not available

A lot of my work is sitting down with the Alameda County Assessor and giving him ideas, then repeating the same idea later on, and pretty soon it becomes a reality. For example, take the county assessing ratio. We didn't like having a 36 percent property tax on inventory.... This is one big achievement for us this year; the county assessor has reduced the ratio on inventory to 28 percent.[57]

Thus business has whittled down its official tax rate over the years until, by 1971, any difference in tax rates between a multimillion dollar corporation and the owner of a $7,000 house in West Oakland will have entirely disappeared, along with any pretense at a progressive tax schedule.

All of the above figures on taxes suffer one serious defect: they deal only with official tax rates, the rates set by state and county law. The actual rate paid by the big corporations is another story, and at this point the political power of the corporations is revealed at the county level. Two situations since 1945, the first a continuing condition of low downtown property assessments, the second a bribery scandal, suggest the continuing ability of medium and large business to avoid high tax rates. We deal here with the only publicized cases of evasion since 1945. There may be other cases that have not come to public attention.

Preferential Treatment? Oakland's Property Tax, 1929-1945

Fractional assessment in Oakland has not meant equal fractions for all. For a period of at least 17 years it meant a sharp reduction of taxes for the large downtown stores and a lesser reduction or increase in taxes for small homeowners and small businessmen. The depression provided the impetus for fractional assessments in general. Without any legislative authority, indeed contrary to the requirements of the California State Constitution, the Oakland city assessor began in 1930 to assess property value in Oakland at a fraction of its real value (see Table 4-8). In 1929 Oakland had a total assessed land value (not including buildings) of over $136 million. By 1945 this same total land value was assessed at about $84 million, a decrease of about $52 million. The total value of the city (land and buildings) dropped about $18 million in the same period. Of course these lower figures did not represent the true market value of Oakland. Over $159 million of building permits were issued for

TABLE 4-8   Tax assessments on major downtown Oakland businesses, 1929-1945

	1929	1933	1944	1945
Tax rate (per $100)	$5.96	$5.06	$5.09	$5.57
Kahns				
Land	$704,000	$468,300	$275,300	$280,300
Improvements	225,600	211,000	211,000	211,000
Hotel Leamington				
Land	114,000	not found	35,600	36,900
Improvements	300,000	not found	243,000	243,000
Central Bank				
Land	462,000	330,975	218,950	225,000
Improvements	650,000	600,000	590,000	590,000
Latham Square Bldg.				
Land	214,000	173,700	108,600	113,200
Improvements	350,000	290,000	275,000	275,000
Athens Athletic Club				
Land	144,650	78,800	44,000	44,000
Improvements	240,000	218,500	200,000	200,000
Block 157				
Land	564,300	398,200	370,700	378,000
Improvements	87,300	81,650	91,650	91,650
Central Bldg. & Loan Assn.				
Land	15,500	11,500	6,000	6,250
Improvements	11,000	13,500	10,000	10,000
Hotel St. Mark				
Land	90,400	54,500	33,550	34,800
Improvements	94,000	45,350	45,350	45,350
Crocker Bank*				
Land	54,100†	30,850	16,000	16,550
Improvements	32,000	28,800	28,800	28,200
Bank of America, 12th and Broadway				
Land	351,750	210,550	137,500	144,000
Improvements	600,000	513,000	513,000	513,000

Source: California *Labor Herald,* May 6, 1946, p. 4.

*Formerly Farmers & Merchants Bank.

†1931 assessment.

Oakland during these years, yet the assessed value of improvements for the city rose only $34 million, or less than one-quarter the amount of the building permits. The result was huge tax savings for property owners. Table 4-8 shows the decline in assessed values for nine major buildings and one block in the downtown area. The total value of these nine buildings and an entire downtown block on Washington Street, Block 157, was about $5.2 million in 1929, and $3.7 million in 1946—a loss of almost $1.5 million, or 25 percent of the 1929 value. That this does not reflect true values should be noted. In 1947, Block 157 was the heart of the city's business district, and was described at that time by Richard Graves, then secretary of the Eastbay division of the California League of Cities as "The hottest business spot in town."[58]

At the same time that the value of the city was being written off the assessor's books, very much like an accelerated tax-depreciation allowance for present-day corporations, taxes on small businesses and home-owners were going down much less rapidly or were actually rising. A comparison of Table 4-9, with two other control blocks in Oakland, reveals the apparent favoritism received by the downtown property owners. In Table 4-9, Block 888 is in East Oakland on 35th Avenue, and is primarily residential. Block 1911 is on MacArthur Boulevard, also in East Oakland, and is primarily small business.

Here we can compare the relative changes between downtown and nondowntown property. While the total assessed value of the 10 down-town stores and blocks was dropping 25 percent between 1929 and 1945 (Table 4-8) the assessed value of land in a small-business block (1911) was rising over 25 percent in the same period, and the value of a residential block (888) was falling only about 7 percent. It is possible that these different rates of change represented actual differences in market values; that the small business area actually did increase, while

TABLE 4-9   *Assessed value of all lots in two blocks in east Oakland, land only*

Year	Block 1911 ($)	Block 888 ($)
1929	30,400	11,250
1945	46,475	10,425

Source: California *Labor Herald*, May 6, 1946, p. 1.

Block 157 actually decreased. But this is not a plausible explanation. Block 1911 in East Oakland, located on a major boulevard, was a neighborhood commercial district, a far less desirable business location during the 1930s and 1940s than the downtown location of buildings shown in Table 4-8, all of whom were in the central business district of the city, the part which was described at the time as "The hottest business spot in town." It seems more likely that the tax assessor gave a bigger tax break to the central business district than to outlying and residential areas.

The results of these discrepant rates can be seen in the value of the tax bills actually paid by these different areas. Tax rates were, in 1931, $5.80; in 1943, $5.24. Table 4-10 shows that the tax bill of small businesses on Block 1911 were up 40 percent after 1929, while taxes on the two major daily newspapers were still below the 1929 figures.

Thus fractional assessments resulted in a much-reduced rate of taxation for downtown businesses and, apparently, a relatively greater tax burden for small businessmen and homeowners. This has had a definite and curtailing effect on the city's budget. In 1946 the city assessor was assessing city business property at about 40 to 50 percent of its actual value. To have assessed it at full value would have meant a bonanza to the city in tax receipts. If downtown Oakland had been paying increases in its tax bills during the Depression and war years as had Block 1911 the city would not have had such a shortage of funds. Oakland, like most American cities, has always been short of public health nurses and public services in general. The failure of the city's major commercial properties to pay taxes at market value, or at the same rates as small homeowners, is a part of the explanation of these shortages.

TABLE 4-10 Comparison of downtown with nondowntown tax bills, selected years, 1929-1946

Year	Post-Inquirer ($)	Oakland Tribune ($)	Block 1911 ($)
1929	13,926.96	54,563.80	4,057.34
1945	6,956.93	37,048.85	*
1946	10,414.23	49,497.75	6,809.40

Source: California *Labor Herald*, May 6, 1946, p. 4.
*Not available

The Scandal of 1966

By 1966 tax collecting in Alameda County was done for most cities, including Oakland, by the county. Corruption in the county assessor's office was exposed in 1966 when a tax consultant admitted bribing the assessor to lower tax rates for several major corporations in the county. Most of the accused were state and national corporations; owners of downtown Oakland properties were not charged. These corporations included Kaiser Center, Inc., Smith-Corona-Marchant, U.S. Plywood, and others. Over fifty businesses in the county had illegally avoided payment of $2,060,888 in county taxes between 1963 and 1966.[59] The power of these corporations is indicated both by the ability to evade legal taxes over these years and their subsequent ability to avoid punishment for evasion. Not a single corporation executive was prosecuted for tax evasion. Only county assessors and tax consultants were prosecuted or jailed in Alameda and San Francisco Counties. The companies denied any knowledge of illegal activity, and the district attorney for Alameda County publicly accepted this disclaimer.

Instead of punishment the corporations are anticipating major tax rewards in the coming years. C. J. Hearn, a retired executive of the Bank of America who became acting county assessor just after the scandal broke, estimated that the new state law which requires that all types of property be assessed at the same rate by 1971 would result in a lowering of taxes paid by commercial and industrial enterprises by $7 million.[60] Such is the anti-penalty that city and county corporations suffer for avoiding payment of over $2 million of taxes in three years' time.

CONCLUSION: INDUSTRIAL POWER
AND CITY HOUSING POLITICS

This chapter has presented evidence on the extent of influence wielded by the real estate industry and Oakland-based corporations over the city's housing policies. Business groups have approved the minimal amounts of public housing actually constructed between 1937 and 1950 and were instrumental in preventing the passage and construction of additional units between 1950 and 1963. Government projects supported by large corporations and local business have caused the demolition of over 8,900 units of low-cost housing between 1955 and 1970. In the area of racial discrimination in housing, the city has filed and forgotten an official study which finds substantial evidence of such discrimination; has dissolved the committee appointed to take action on the report; and has placed public housing in ghetto and industrial areas of the city. It rescinded its rent control laws under pressure from real estate interests. Its building, heating and ventilating, plumbing, and housing codes are written in large part by the industry itself. The housing code enforcement program is, by admission of city officials, incapable of doing more than "hold the line" on code violations, while the stiffest enforcement procedure of the new code was deleted from the legislation at the insistence of the Oakland Real Estate Board. In short the basic policies of city and county government are guided so as either not to hurt, or to give financial assistance to, private real estate and industrial interests. In only one instance—passage of a code enforcement act—did the writer find something done by the city which was opposed by the real estate industry. But this act was passed, not as a concession to a democratic ground swell, but at the suggestion of the powerful corporate officials sitting on OCCUR. And in the upshot the final code enforcement ordinance contained so many concessions to slum owners that code enforcement has become a semifarce. Far from solving the housing problems of the poor and working people of the city, government projects and policies have compounded these problems to the benefit of the government treasury and the owners of property.

NOTES

1. *Northern California Real Estate Report,* 3d Quarter, 1965, p. 52.
2. Governor's Advisory Commission on Housing Problems (Eichler Commission), *Housing in California* (summary), 1963, p. 40.
3. "(The proposed bill) was bitterly fought by the savings and loan associations, the banks and other financial interests. The measure passed the Assembly but was dumped in the Senate . . . in response to the opposition of the community of financial groups opposing it." Source: California Labor Federation (AFL-CIO), *The Sacramento Story, Labor and the Legislature,* 1963.
4. The Oakland Veterans Council, composed of representatives of 53 community organizations, was put off by the city council at least four times. See San Francisco *Labor Herald,* January 24, 1947.

5. Alameda County Council of Social Planning, "The Case for Additional Low-Income Public Housing in Oakland, California," July 21, 1966, p. 4.

6. Oakland Housing Authority, *Sixth Annual Report,* 1946, p. 14.

7. Oakland City Council Resolution #24145 CMS, January 24, 1950.

8. The projects: Westwood Gardens (46 units); Chestnut Court (77); Palo Vista Gardens (100); San Antonio Villa (178); and Tassaforanga Village (105).

9. "Further, boxcars; vacant buildings, houses, doorways, automobiles provide shelter. . . . Hobohemias have existed along the railroad tracks." Source: Council of Economic Planning, *Report No. 76, Study of Missions in Oakland, California,* 1965, p. 9.

10. (Oakland Chamber of Commerce) *Outlook,* August 1959, p. 10.

11. In West Oakland along Fifth Street, BART paid under $10,000 for nine of about forty houses which it bought and demolished, approximately 40 percent of all houses on this street. Source: BART census tract maps and figures.

12. BART'S change of policy was due to the public outcry against the earlier practice of no assistance.

13. California *Labor Herald,* January 24, 1947, p. 3.

14. For a perceptive discussion of the ideological bases of opposition to public housing, see Leonard Freedman, *Public Housing, The Politics of Poverty,* New York: Holt, 1969, esp. chap. 5.

15. Letter from F. D. Courneen, President of Oakland Real Estate Board, dated 31 March 1938; quoted in Oakland City Planning Commission, "Need for a Low Rent Housing Project in Oakland, California," April 5, 1938.

16. The 1937 Housing Act, as amended in 1949, states that the Federal government shall not assist a local public housing agency to build public housing "unless the public housing agency has demonstrated that a gap of at least 20 per centum . . . has been left between the proposed low-rent housing and the lowest rents at which private enterprise is providing (housing)." "U.S. Housing Act of 1937," in *Basic Laws and Authorities on Housing and Urban Development* (as revised through January 31, 1970), Committee on Banking and Currency, U.S. House of Representatives, 91st Congress 2d Sess., Washington: GPO, 1970, p. 250.

17. Oakland Chamber of Commerce, *The Metropolitan,* June 1, 1943, p. 1.

18. The following information on Oakland's housing politics from 1960 through 1966 comes from Edward Horwinsky, retired Executive Secretary of the Oakland Housing Authority, interview October 15, 1966.

19. Interview, March 1968.

20. Oakland Housing Authority, *Eighth Annual Report,* 1948, p. 5

21. The Agreement states in part: "The city undertakes and agrees that . . . there has been or will be equivalent elimination of unsafe or unsanitary dwelling units in compliance with the provisions of Section 10-a of the (1937 Housing) Act."

22. (Oakland Housing Authority) *Newsletter,* April 1966, p. 3.

23. Ibid.
24. Floyd Hunter, *Housing Discrimination in Oakland, California* (Oakland, 1964).
25. Acts of omission are identical to Peter Bachrach's "non-decisions". See Peter Bachrach and Morton Baratz, *Power and Poverty, Theory and Practice,* New York: Oxford University, 1970.
26. Hunter, op. cit.
27. Committee on Full Opportunity (COFO), *Report on Discrimination in Housing in Oakland, California,* June 7, 1965, p. 1.
28. Ibid., p. 6.
29. Oakland *Tribune,* January 18, 1966, p. 1.
30. A term employed in the report by Floyd Hunter, op. cit.
31. Oakland Housing Authority, *Report,* 1958, passim.
32. Leon Henderson, Director, U.S. Office of Rent Stabilization, *A Report on Stabilization of Rents in the United States,* Washington: GPO, 1953, p. 1.
33. In the Leamington Hotel, Oakland's leading hotel, rents soared: on the tenth floor, rent in one room went from $50 to $136; on the third floor, another room increased from $40 to $100; another went from $50 to 135; yet another from $50 to $150. See *Labor Herald,* July 22, 1947, p. 3.
34. Robert Snell, President, Alameda County Apartment House Owners Association, telephone conversation, July 16, 1968.
35. Oakland City Council, *Public Hearings on Rent Decontrol,* August 23, 1951, p. 43.
36. Oakland *Tribune,* August 24, 1951. See also Area Rent Office Personnel, Alameda County Defense Rental Area, *Housing Vacancy Survey, Oakland, California,* Oakland, August 20, 1951, passim.
37. Oakland City Council, *Minutes,* September 13, 1951.
38. Council of Social Planning (Oakland), "The Case for Additional Low-income Public Housing," July 1966, p. 9.
39. Mr. Lawrence Lane, Oakland Department of Housing, interview September 1966.
40. Ibid.
41. (Oakland Chamber of Commerce) *Outlook,* October 21, 1948.
42. *Outlook,* September 1949.
43. *Outlook,* October 1950.
44. Enrico Labarberra, Oakland housing department official, interview, December 19, 1966.
45. Resolution adopted by OCCUR (1957), on file, Oakland City Clerk.
46. Oakland City Council, *Minutes,* September 17, 1957.
47. Letter from Fred Squires to Oakland City Council, September 18, 1957.
48. Building Code of the City of Oakland.
49. E. Labarberra, interview cited.
50. "Report to the City Council and Mayor Clifford Rishell from Wayne Thompson, City Manager", January 7, 1958.

51. Oakland *Tribune* February 14, 1966, p. 1.

52. California (State) Assembly Interim Committee on Revenue and Taxation, *California's Tax Structure 1964*, January, 1964, part 1, p. 19.

53. Of the 1962 local property tax total, $634 million was collected by counties, $409 million by cities, $1.18 million by school districts and roughly $212 million by other special districts, a total of about $2.4 billion. The Federal government, in the same year, collected $9.4 billion in taxes from California. Ibid.

54. Richard Musgrave, "The Incidence of the Tax Structure and its Effects on Consumption," *Federal Tax Policy for Economic Growth*, Joint Committee on the Economic Report, Washington: GPO, 1956, p. 98. See also Dick Netzer, *Economics of the Property Tax*, Washington: Brookings, 1966; and James Maxwell, *Financing State and Local Governments*, Washington: Brookings, 1969.

55. Testimony of Gerhard N. Rostvold, Ph.D., of Pomona College; in hearings before the Assembly Interim Committee on Revenue and Taxation, 1964, Vol. 5, p. 306.

56. Constitution of the State of California, sec. 12, art. XI.

57. Interview, August 1966. The Alameda County Taxpayers Association (ACTA) is largely supported by big business. Included on the Association's roster of officers in 1966 were executives from General Motors, Pacific Gas and Electric, Pacific Telephone, Shell Oil, General Electric, and Caterpillar Tractor. Source: (ACTA) *News Facts*, May 18, 1966, p. 1.

58. California *Labor Herald*, May 24, 1946, p. 3.

59. Oakland *Tribune*, February 24, 1966, p. 4.

60. Oakland *Tribune*, September 15, 1966, p. 13.

CHAPTER FIVE

Urban Redevelopment:

Corporate Welfare and Black Revolt

The postwar planning committee did not deal with the question of the city's physical renewal, a problem almost as severe as the shortage of public services. In 1945 California passed its first community redevelopment law which allowed city councils to create redevelopment agencies, and to give these agencies the powers of eminent domain, bonding, and borrowing from state or Federal authority.[1] The new law was not greeted with much enthusiasm by California businessmen. In effect it enabled the state to take private property for private redevelopment and become the instrument for one property group driving out others. As a result the local response to the new law was cautious. In Richmond, an industrial suburb just north of Oakland and Berkeley, redevelopment projects 10 years after the law was passed were in areas occupied by temporary war housing or owned by the Federal government. Private property was not touched. Los Angeles and San Francisco were the first cities to create redevelopment agencies, each in 1948, three years after the Law's passage. Six other cities had followed suit by 1955, but San Diego, a major metropolitan area, still had none as of that year. Rural areas were even slower to set up redevelopment agencies, despite the fact that almost as much substandard housing exists in rural as central city areas.

The need for redevelopment of the downtown area arose from the absence of recent downtown construction, and from property management practices. While Oakland was expanding rapidly, before and after the First World War, almost all of its present stock of Class A downtown office buildings were completed, including the Tribune Tower (completed 1924), the Financial Center Building (1915), and the Bank of America (1911). There have been only five new major buildings built in downtown Oakland in the past 40 years, while most of the new smaller buildings since 1940 have been in a downtown area somewhat north of the old Washington Street commercial core, a process of business district bifurcation which has divided the city's downtown property owners politically and contributed substantially to the economic decline of the older, southerly commercial area.

The practices of property owners have also been a source of difficulty for the city. Many downtown owners have refused to sell property to the city for use as parking lots, leaving the city with a relatively limited supply of downtown parking. Most of the present owners of downtown buildings either built their properties themselves or are the children of the builders, and can see no reason to sell, especially if the city intends the property for such a mundane purpose as parking. One member of the city's downtown parking commission wryly commented, "We could use a few funerals in this town."

The overriding pressure for urban renewal was the exodus of the white middle-class homeowners, of whom an estimated 100,000 left the city between 1950 and 1960, and their replacement by low income, largely black and Chicano renters whose presence in the city has galled the downtown merchants. Washington Street in nearby West Oakland, once the major shopping avenue, now caters to a largely poor clientele. Between 1959 and 1965 vacancies in the downtown area rose to a phenomenal 21 percent, while in the five years 1958-1963 a total of 80 businesses went bankrupt or simply left town.[2]

The General Neighborhood Renewal Plan, the city's first broad plan for redevelopment, was introduced in 1957 largely to save the remaining downtown merchants from total economic eclipse. All housing in the renewal plan's first clearance project, Acorn, was planned at middle-income rent levels.

Simply by taking all the units out of the price category which the poor can afford it was hoped to assure a higher-income class of tenants. According to one downtown merchant his fellow merchants would have liked to have had an even higher median rent for Acorn housing but realized the difficulty of getting even medium-income people to move into a small project area in the midst of a larger slum. At the same time Acorn has planned a very low number of efficiency units for the elderly. Acorn would be an ideal location for the elderly because it is very close to the downtown shopping area and would permit walking to downtown by the elderly, who could thereby save transportation expenses. But older people are a bad market. Over half of those in Alameda County over 65 years of age receive less than $1,000 annual income, so there will be few units built for them in Acorn. One agency report puts the matter succinctly: "Oakland's central business district is expected to benefit from this higher per capita purchasing power for consumer goods resulting from the renewal of Oak Center . . . Acorn and Corridor projects."

At the same time the action taken by the city itself prior to urban renewal went a long way toward creating the necessity for renewal.[3] Shortly after publication of the General Neighborhood Renewal Plan in 1957, the Department of Building and Housing sent a letter to the residents of West Oakland stating that the city had plans to "do something" with the area. As a result of this letter, according to a member of the redevelopment agency staff, the people of far west Oakland began to look at their neighborhood as something temporary. Why fix up your house if the city was going to demolish it anyway? was the attitude. People began to move out of West Oakland—indeed the population figures for that part of the city have dropped substantially over the past decade, while rising or remaining constant in all other parts of the city—and efforts at home repair declined. By the early 1960s leading institutions were practicing what amounted to a "freeze" in home repair funds for this area, making credit all but unobtainable in the blocks west of MacArthur Freeway.

Federal loans to homeowners were also held up during the 1960s. According to Mr. Wade Johnson, longtime resident of the city and president of the United Taxpayers and Voters Union, "There was $50 million in Federal money available from the Federal Housing Administration for low-interest loans and with twenty-five years for repayment ready if the City Council would give the green light."[4] But the council never did. A $1,500 Federal grant, promised in October of 1966 to poor homeowners for home repair, had still not materialized as of April 1967. The letter from the Department of Building and Housing, the credit freeze, and the withholding of all Federal funds needed for home rehabilitation all tended to force West Oakland into physical decline. Credit starvation for 10 years can injure the most prosperous residential area; it can ruin an area already starting to become a slum. Even with the small amounts of money made available by the Model Cities program for rehabilitation, West Oakland has continued on a course of physical decline for which some amount of demolition has become a practical necessity.

This complementary activity of public and private agencies in the redevelopment area meets the tests of pluralist theory for pluralist policy making, because of the numerous political actors who played important roles. The downtown financial institutions limited or denied access of West Oakland to private mortgage credit. The city council was unwilling to take advantage of possible Federal relief; the California legislature created the legal basis for the city's urban renewal agency; and several Federal departments have been active in creating and executing renewal policy. In addition, the local school board and the county board of supervisors have been involved in redevelopment plans, and a business-dominated private citizens committee has maintained a constant policy involvement. This is pluralism par excellence. But it has led in one direction: the eviction of the tenant poor and small businessmen. Only with the entry of an organization which united the neighborhoods *against* city activity did local residents have an effective voice. The crucial fact about this new organization, the West Oakland Planning Council (WOPC) was its ideology, its independence from downtown businesses and political groups, and its organic relationship to the local neighborhoods (see pp. 123-125). With the organization of the WOPC a genuine pluralism entered the picture for the first time.

RENEWAL PROGRAMS AND DOMINANT POLITICAL FORCES

Oakland's Redevelopment, 1949-1957

The city's first steps toward redevelopment resulted in a fiasco. In June of 1949 the planning commission prepared a report on the possibilities of redevelopment, entitled "Blight in Our City." The report included, in black ink, a large area designated by the report as blighted, including parts of downtown and the non-slum district east of Lake Merritt. This report produced such a storm from local property owners that, on

January 17, 1950, the city council passed a resolution stating that, in fact, there was no blight in the city.

Yet the facts were too omnipresent to be dispelled even by resolution of the city council. Late in 1953 the city planning commission again took up the question of redevelopment, and in 1954, Oakland's economic elite began to champion the cause. This support gave a new face to the matter, and it is to this period of the program that we now turn.

Creation of OCCUR The history of industrial involvement in the city's redevelopment programs begins in 1952. In that year the city's real estate board, acting in its capacity as unofficial policy maker, brought Mr. William Morris up from Los Angeles to discuss the Los Angeles experience. At about the same time the president of the Oakland Apartment House Owners Association led a committee for one year on the subject of redevelopment. Neither of these efforts resulted in any substantial accomplishment. In 1954 John Houlihan, onetime libel lawyer for the *Tribune,* was elected mayor and appointed a new dynamic committee of redevelopment supporters. On this new committee were certain key figures necessary to get redevelopment moving: the executive vice-president of the Homebuilders Association of the East Bay, the past and present presidents of the Oakland Real Estate Board, a corporation attorney active in local politics, and a leading official of a major downtown department store.

The early operation of the committee is described by the past president of the city's real estate board in these words:

> The five of us met at the Athens Athletic Club and organized a citizens committee. We decided we needed a full-time chairman, so we went to Kaiser Industries and got Norris Nash.
>
> We appointed our own steering committee, which met at the executive quarters of the Kaiser Building on Wednesday mornings. We advised Norris on the kind of programs we wanted to undertake. Then the whole committee met on Friday mornings for meetings of the full committee of 25 members.[5]

The Friday breakfast meetings of the citizens committee have continued every week of every year to the present. Until a city redevelopment agency was created in 1957, the Citizens Committee for Urban

Renewal (which later added the word Oakland and adopted the abbreviated title OCCUR) exercised semigovernmental powers in the creation and direction of urban renewal activity, and succeeded ultimately in pushing the city council into adopting much of the program which it desired. Rarely in Oakland's postwar history has a single private group had such important control over so extensive a project.

OCCUR rapidly became the contact point for business and governmental groups involved in the process of urban renewal. Such a broadening of participation was required by the fact that urban redevelopment has cut across broad sections of Oakland's political and economic infrastructure, requiring new school facilities, rerouting of surface level streets, relocation of businesses, etc. OCCUR functioned to gain public and private support for redevelopment and to coordinate the various activities of the program.

The main feature of OCCUR's activity has been a weekly breakfast meeting, during which sympathetic business and government executives could acquire the intimate knowledge necessary for understanding and correctly planning redevelopment projects. At the one meeting of OCCUR which this author attended the superintendent of the local junior college district reported on the recent successful bond election for his district and on the planning that had been done in connection with the new junior college site to be located in the Civic Center (downtown) redevelopment project area. His plans included the demolition of the Exposition Building, locating the Rapid Transit tracks underground, closing Eight Street entirely, and working with the newly created flood control district which was planning to create a small lake on the new campus.

Thus accurate information on major policy decisions was presented at this meeting. In good measure it has been the exchange of this kind of information which has made OCCUR a major center of power.

It should also be noted that access to such information was restricted to a select group. All of those in attendance at the meeting attended by this writer were either local businessmen, property owners, or officials of local government agencies. There were no community blacks, small businessmen, or wage earners. In 1959, when OCCUR's membership was published in the appendix of an urban renewal report, the committee included on it an impressive array of the economic elite, including, among others, three representatives from Kaiser Industries, one each from Sears Roebuck, Equitable Life Assurance Company, and Wells Fargo Bank. Two of the businesses represented—Kaiser Industries and the Bank of America—had a total combined net worth in 1971 of over \$4 billion. The committee included a scattering of housewives and ministers, so that the word "citizens" in its name (Citizens Committee for Urban Renewal) would not appear entirely inappropriate.

In 1969 a militant group of the city's Negroes, the Oakland Black Caucus, protested to the San Francisco office of the U.S. Department of Housing and and Urban Development (HUD) that OCCUR, contrary to the guidelines of HUD for a citizen's committee, was composed almost totally of businessmen and was quite unrepresentative of the city. The director of HUD in San Francisco agreed with the complaint and refused certification of the city's workable program until OCCUR was reconstituted, a move which threatened to hold up Federal renewal funds for the city.[6]

The first Battle of Oakland The citizens committee began by drawing up a comprehensive program for the entire city of Oakland, which would have placed every building in the city under some renewal program, from outright demolition or rehabilitation for the most decayed areas to a simple conservation plan for the better-preserved parts of the city. But the city council, whose membership was almost identical to the council which passed the "no blight" resolution in 1950, rejected the plan. The council, in refusing to accept demolition aspects of OCCUR's plan, seemed to be anticipating popular opposition to any further breaking up of Oakland neighborhoods by demolition projects. The Battle of Oakland was underway.

The rejection by the city council of the OCCUR plan for comprehensive redevelopment and conservation of the city represented a continuation of established council policy. But now that policy was facing opposition from those who had the technique, the finances, and the national support to batter it down.[7] Between 1954 and 1957 OCCUR began a massive campaign to popularize redevelopment and put the city council on the defensive. During this period ACTION, the national organization of large real estate developers who supported redevelopment, sent its president, Major General Frederick A. Irving, to confer with Oakland officials in connection with the first redevelopment project in Oakland, Clinton Parks, to "provide information and assistance on the project." The junior chamber of commerce, working with a committee of the chamber headed by Robert W. Turner (Kaiser Industries) and Culver Wold (Equitable Life Assurance Company), prepared a film on urban renewal in the Clinton Park area that was shown to "more than 50 civic, church, school and women's organizations,"[8] by early 1957. Officials of the Department of Building and Housing gave, by their own accounting, dozens of talks to church service and business groups, popularizing the idea of redevelopment. Thus the citizens committee, unable to budge the council on the first try, began to mold public opinion with the help of a friendly local governmental department.

One lagging sector of public opinion in Oakland was the business community itself. During the 1950s urban renewal had only partial support from this community on the national level, while at the local level businessmen were not eager to support an untried program which required heavy involvement with government planners. Hence OCCUR began a campaign to win over local businessmen to the program. Between 1954 and 1957 dozens of Federal officials visited Oakland to promote redevelopment. Articles began appearing in the local monopoly* paper favorable to the renewal concept, and pointing out the long-standing hazardous conditions of housing in West Oakland.

During this same period Andrew Heiskell, then publisher of *Life Magazine,* gave a talk on the advantages of renewal to some 200 leading industrialists, businessmen and public officials at a meeting arranged by the chamber of commerce:

> Urban renewal has a practical business side. . . . slums mean crime and social problems and to a businessman who pays so much taxes this is important. . . . The plain fact is that people living in bad housing do not make good customers. Obviously no running water means no plumbing supplies; those whose houses are unpainted and dirty have little incentive to buy carpets or curtains.

> It is not obvious but still true, that those who become used to such housing standards are not likely to demand higher standards in food, clothing, books, and entertainment and a host of other things contributing to the ever-higher economy our way of life requires.[9]

*The term "monopoly" is used here because, while the city has several tabloid papers and sells the daily San Francisco paper, no daily paper has published in Oakland in competition with the *Tribune* since 1953.

As an additional part of its campaign OCCUR organized a bus tour of West Oakland slums for city councilmen and other officials, a tour which produced front page discoveries in the *Tribune* of rats and terrible housing conditions.[10] Finally, to persuade reluctant officials and businessmen, the Kaiser and Bechtel companies chartered a private airplane and took the mayor, the whole city council, and a *Tribune* reporter on a trip to several eastern cities where urban renewal was already in progress. The *Tribune* reporter sent back dispatches which were prominently displayed in the pages of his newspaper.

By 1957 OCCUR's campaign to win over city officials, civic groups, and local businessmen was bearing fruit. Its proposal for a centralized department of public safety was turned down by the city council. But the General Neighborhood Renewal Plan was being prepared by the planning commission; a "citizens" subcommittee of affected businessmen was preparing the new code enforcement ordinance which passed the city council in November of 1957; and the council—yielding to the pressures of three years of diligent work by OCCUR—appointed itself as redevelopment agency for the city and began the first redevelopment project. Thus a combine of local businessmen and national officials, aided by the local monopoly paper, overcame the politicians' objections and the public's inertia to win the first, and most important, battle for renewal.

The Urban Renewal and Model Cities Programs in Action, 1957-1970

Clinton Parks The first program which the city council undertook was the Clinton Parks area, a 78-block area of lingering middle-class housing which, while deteriorating, was still salvageable. In this neighborhood the council undertook a code enforcement program. No financial assistance was offered to homeowners who were told, in effect, to repair or lose their property. As stated in a report by the Oakland Renewal Foundation, a private group supporting the project:

> A major problem (of the Clinton Parks project) was the lack of financial assistance needed by property owners. The Oakland Renewal Foundation had been created to meet this need, but it lacked the funds."[11]

The ORF report also made clear that the project "did not provide for relocation assistance to families moving from the site." But for local businesses in the area, the program was quite useful. Safeway Stores, a large California food chain, acquired an entire city block in the area and erected a $193,000 supermarket; another company erected a 144-unit apartment building with cheap FHA financing previously used only by low-income homeowners who could not afford the market rate of interest.[12] A 78 Block Club of homeowners in the Clinton Parks area held meetings and circulated a petition of protest but was unsuccessful in stopping or amending the project.

General Neighborhood Renewal Plan (GNRP), Acorn, and Oak Center The GNRP, drawn up in 1957, represented a much greater victory for OCCUR. The new plan designated five urban renewal projects in the West Oakland area, a total of 225 acres. It also called for demolition. A planner in the redevelopment agency remarked to this writer, in 1967, that OCCUR played a leading role in the creation of the larger plan.

Between 1957 and 1971 the GNRP area has changed somewhat. One area in far West Oakland was dropped, another closer to downtown was added, along with the new Civic Center project, the latter an elaborate plan for the complete rebuilding of the downtown area. The Model Cities program in deep West Oakland was added in 1966 and covers an area about as large as the original 225-acre GNRP. The city chose to begin these new projects in the Acorn area.

The figures which the renewal agency itself developed for Acorn indicate a willingness to destroy sound structures. According to the GNRP, 59 percent of all structures in Acorn were "substandard" according to "modified APHA techniques". This figure represents the percentage of structures which, by the agency's definition, were beyond rehabilitation and in need of demolition as of 1957. The subgroupings of the plan divided Acorn into seven subdistricts and gave the percentage of structures needing demolition in each of these subdistricts. In two of the seven districts 70 percent or more of the structures were substandard, but in the other five districts about 60 percent *or more* of the total structures were designated *standard*. Thus only two subdistricts were real "offenders" according to the agency's own figures and techniques. Yet in the first five years of renewal bulldozers demolished *every* standing structure in the Acorn area, with the exception of a mortuary, a church, and one house used as the agency field office.

Eight years of meticulous and expensive planning by the redevelopment agency and planning department led to the demolition of 333 structures classfied as standard by the renewal agency 10 years earlier. This lesson was not lost on the black population of West Oakland and accounts, in part, for the militant tactics of the present Black Caucus and West Oakland Planning Council.

The fate of Acorn sparked some popular opposition to urban renewal in the second GNRP area, Oak Center, beginning in 1962. Because of this community protest the agency director employed a two-pronged strategy. Publicly he told the people of the project area that Oak Center would be largely rehabilitation, and only secondarily demolition (80 percent: 20 percent). Yet according to several reports from persons connected with the agency at that time, the director was simultaneously planning the entire area for 80 percent demolition and telling this version to the urban renewal administration in San Francisco. This double policy caused considerable friction among staff members within the agency, many of whom resigned. Finally an official from the San Francisco office of HUD went to the Oakland City Council and complained. The council fired the director. But the result has not been a victory for candor. In 1968 the Oakland agency was still planning to demolish 1,900 of the 2,749 dwelling *units* in Oak Center, or about 75 percent, while publicly maintaining the somewhat misleading position that out of 1097 *structures* in the project area, 450—almost 50 percent—would be rehabilitated.[13] Thus the people of Oak Center were programmed for much the same fate as the people of Acorn.

Model Cities: more of the same? In its latest neighborhood project, the Model Cities area in deep West Oakland, the agency has again promised to walk softly. In its plans for a four-block prototype project within the larger project area, it stated that "Development programs should minimize displacement while concentrating on innovative rehabilitation techniques."[14] But no definite figures were given in this report and, indeed, figures included in the report indicated that 40 percent of the families in the Model Cities area are too poor to qualify for rehabilitation loans. All such families who are homeowners, by implication, may be moved when the program begins.[15] The report leaves open the possibility that all properties in the area will be purchased by the agency. If this should happen then the agency *could,* if it wished, demolish every structure it buys in the area with no legal avenue of redress by the previous owners.

What is surprising about this report is the strong case which it presents for rehabilitation of even the more deteriorated houses. The agency uses a scale for rehabilitation and grades houses according to their condition. Condition 1 means the structure meets the requirements of the building code. Condition 2 means market value of the house must be spent to bring it up to the requirements of the building code. Condition 3 means that 25 to 50 percent of the market value must be spent to bring the house up to the requirements of the code, and Condition 4 means that over 50 percent of the market value must be spent. The report then gives the results of its survey showing how many units fall into each category:[16]

Condition	No. of units
1	—
2	59
3	96
4	42

The report states subsequently that all of the units in condition 4, representing 21.2 percent of all units in the project area, will be demolished. For the remaining three-quarters of all units, rehabilitation cost would be 50 percent or less of their market value. If market value and replacement value are the same dollar amount, then rehabilitation for these remaining units would be half as cheap at the most as new construction. The report goes on to quote a study by Arthur D. Little Co. for the city of San Francisco, which study, according to the report

indicated that rehabilitation is less expensive than new units. . . . to rehabilitate a one-bedroom unit from Condition 4 (needing extensive repairs and some replacement) to a market condition given normal code enforcement would cost approximately $11,585. The same unit reproduced new would range in price from $15,400 to $25,600. As the size of the unit increases, the difference between the cost of rehabilitation and new housing substantially increases in favor of the former.

The Little study later states:

> A review of brokers indicates that the least expensive units produced in the Bay Area average $15,000 (including land). In the Oakland Acorn project, the average unit-cost in the 221D3 project (low-interest federal loans for new units) is nearly $14,500.[17]

What this suggests is that it would cost less to rehabilitate the *whole* Model Cities area than it will cost to demolish. Yet 21.2 percent is already slated for demolition. What will happen to those owners who are too poor to qualify for loans but whose houses are good enough to rehabilitate? Through its powers of eminent domain the city could simply buy the houses, evict the residents, and either rehabilitate or sell to middle-income families who can afford rehabilitation or middle-income rents. What makes all of this so infuriating for the present residents is that, as the report itself candidly states, the setting of cost figures for deciding between demolition or rehabilitation is not simply a matter of market costs but an act of policy in which the discretion of the agency is involved. The report implies strongly that the agency sets its figures to accord with its own preference for demolition: "A land and unit writedown, if operative for present owners and renters, would permit the successful rehabilitation of most units."[18]

No writedown, or granting of subsidies, for current owners or renters has ever been done in Oakland, although it was done on a broad scale for corporate buyers on cleared land in Acorn, after the original owners were removed (see p. 121). It is not projected for the Model Cities area, and to the knowledge of this writer it has never been a feature of urban renewal anywhere in the country. Removal of the poor is a matter of policy.

An Urban Renewal Scorecard

The poor The poor themselves have shouldered a disproportionate amount of the cost of their own removal because local taxes fall more heavily on the poor than on the other income groups in the city. Over 9,000 residents were forced to relocate by the Acorn project, while those remaining suffered from the fact that the city's greatest postwar spending program did not attack the fundamental problems of jobs, income, and poverty. The poor of the city in general, and of the redevelopment areas in particular, have gained nothing from the completed renewal projects.

Downtown merchants Ironically, the downtown merchants, who were intended to be major beneficiaries of the program, have not come close to realizing their original goals. Urban redevelopment has been slow; while it has succeeded, as of 1971, in moving thousands of low-income customers away from the immediate downtown area, only a few hundred middle-class family replacements have moved back into redeveloped land of the Acorn project. Since this project is located in the heart of a ghettoized area it is of limited attractiveness to many middle-class families. The very fact of low residential density in the new project reduced the number of potential customers for downtown goods and services.

Finally, the objectives of the agency and downtown merchants have occasionally diverged. In 1966 the agency unveiled its City Center redevelopment project which initially called for the possible leveling of over 70 blocks of downtown Oakland and the rebuilding of this area with ultramodern skyscrapers and department stores. Prior to 1966 all redevelopment projects had been aimed at poor residential areas. Mr. Warren Isaacs, Manager of the Downtown Property Owners Association and a longtime supporter of redevelopment, protested to the agency, noting that the new project area included the Tribune Tower, Bank of America Building, Union Trust Building, First Western Building (completed around 1960, an ultramodern high-rise bank and office building), and several structures belonging to the telephone company. His letter commented that "These blocks have the highest assessed value in Oakland's Core district, and to include them (in urban redevelopment) would seem to be a mockery of the alleged purpose of redevelopment."[19]

Perhaps as a result of this protest, the agency no longer publicly discusses any broadscale demolition program for the central business district. But Mr. Isaacs' protest was only partially accurate. Demolition of downtown was a perversion of the original goal of attracting middle-income families close to the downtown area. The destruction of sound structures already had ample precedent in the Acorn project.

Direct benefits to industry For big corporations urban renewal has already proven its worth. Where once a school and low-cost homes stood in Acorn, now Mack Truck, Ford Motor Company, and United States Plywood have attractive new plants surrounded by big parking lots and high fences. The land was sold to them at sharply reduced rates, because the agency has been ready to offer cleared land for half or less its market value. Present holders of property—absentee, for over half the structures in West Oakland—are paid the full market value, as determined by an appraiser. The site is then cleared, new utilities and streets put in if necessary, and sold back to industry at a price reduced enough to attract purchasers. In Oakland there is a substantial differential between the price the agency pays for land, and the price it charges its industrial customers, as is shown in Table 5-1 below. Thus the city—which refuses to write down the unit and land prices for homeowners to make rehabilitation possible—has reduced the price to industry of the same land to about 55 percent of its market value, resulting in what the agency itself calls a subsidy of over $33 million.

Direct benefits to banking industry Banks have bid multimillion dollar bond issues for Oakland redevelopment projects for interest rates ranging from 2.89 and 3.05 percent, rates guaranteed by the Federal government no matter what the outcome of the project. In Oakland in the month of January of 1967 the agency sold a note for $6,750,000 to

TABLE 5-1 Differentials between buying and selling prices of redevelopment project land, six projects

Project	Bought ($)	Sold ($)	Subsidy ($)
Acorn	11,481,000	5,250,000	6,261,000
Oak Center	12,400,000	4,910,000	9,490,000
Corridor	14,574,000	10,655,000	3,919,000
Civic Center-Peralta	19,904,000	11,140,000	8,764,000
Telegraph Sq.	10,953,000	5,500,000	5,453,000
Chinese community	6,368,000	4,500,000	1,868,000
Total	$75,680,000	$41,955,000	$35,755,000

Source: Oakland Redevelopment Agency, *A Report on Current Activities,* April 21, 1965, *passim.*

the First National Bank of Boston, at a 2.89 percent rate of interest, to finance work in the Acorn project. That interest rate will yield $195,075 in accrued interest in a single year for a single bank for this single project, in addition to which the bank is entitled to charge a 1.5 percent service fee against the Federal government when it resells the note to the Federal National Mortgage Association.[20] Thus banks, plus several major corporations, plus a cast of hundreds of small business-men in Oakland are waiting to capture all the direct economic benefits of redevelopment. These same business interests have demonstrated their own ability, in the Civic Center project, to stop a demolition plan injurious to their interests; yet when the agency removed 9,000 poor from the West End, with relocation assistance of $200 per capita, these same interests maintained a most influential silence. Perhaps the name of the program could be changed from urban renewal to business renewal; for it is not the city as a whole which is being enhanced, but the economic fortunes and investment opportunities of local merchants and locally based larger corporations.

PARTICIPATION, STRUGGLE, AND COMMUNITY CONTROL

Since the poverty program, and more specifically since the demand for community control of schools at Ocean Hill-Brownsville, a literature has grown up debating the merits of reform under the slogans of participation and community control.[21] The experience of the city's redevelopment programs provides us with two instances of neighbor-hood organization, one mildly participatory and the other militant and struggle-oriented. Contrasting the experience of these two groups helps to distinguish between meaningful and cooptive forms of neighborhood political involvement and helps answer the question of how much community control is possible within the present political system.

We can begin by looking at the kind of neighborhood control intended by the agency's own directing board. Of its early directors, none came from the target areas; instead the mayor appointed a middle-class housewife, a top official of the county central labor council, a self-employed lawyer who was previously President of the Council of Social Planning and a lower executive of Kaiser Industries. By the late 1960s three new people had been appointed: the owner of a stationery store, a retired executive of the Bank of America, and a retired official of the Oakland *Tribune.* All of the above, with one exception, lived outside all the projected redevelopment areas. At no time did the city council, mayor, planning, or police departments (who all raised objections to various parts of the programs) raise objections to the agency's treatment of the people in the renewal areas;[22] their criticisms were confined to technical aspects of implementation. The agency itself made only very limited efforts to involve target area residents in decision making until the Federal government applied pressure and the neighborhoods organized themselves around a set of demands.

The Oak Center Neighborhood Association (OCNA) was the first stable neighborhood group organized around the problems of redevelopment. The OCNA was a homeowners association set up in the Oak Center project area by the local council of social planning. The association preempted any serious indigenous opposition to the Oak Center program by seeking, within a framework of support for the Oak Center renewal plan, to protect the welfare of the area residents who would be affected. It apparently delayed the demolition of units in Oak Center, although it never publicized the full extent of agency demolition plans. It is an association of home *owners,* whose economic status is above the average in the West Oakland area. OCNA never organized tenants. As one close observer wrote, "At first the Agency disliked the OCNA but finally realized its utility."[23]

By contrast, decision power gained by the West Oakland Planning Council (WOPC), whose tactics have been aggressive and independent, have been substantial. WOPC held its first organizational meeting in December 1967. Because of the broad diversity of groups and opinions in the West Oakland area, WOPC was designed by its leaders as a congress to which every organization in the area, from churches to political parties, could have two elected representatives. Because all could join and vote on election of the steering committee, the WOPC succeeded in uniting the West Oakland area, a unity which played a major role in strengthening the organization's hand during bargaining sessions with city hall. Within a year its membership had grown to 165 organizations, all pulling together, including groups as diverse as the West End Nursery and the Black Panther Party.[24]

Building on the experience of the poverty program, whose militant director Mr. Percy Moore provided useful assistance, the WOPC began with a high-level series of demands, including demands for control over the appointment of the Model Cities program director; direct access to the city council; the channelling of all model cities funds from the city council to WOPC, which would act as the neighborhood planning council for Model Cities; and the right to veto all Model Cities programs.[25] The mayor, City Council, and *Tribune* all objected strenuously. The result was a compromise which still gave WOPC a very strong position. Instead of WOPC as the neighborhood planning council, the compromise called for an independent Model Cities Policy Committee on which WOPC had 51 percent of the votes. It allowed the Model Cities director to be appointed by the city manager from a list of nominees submitted by a six-man panel, three of whose members would be appointed by WOPC. Study committees would be appointed for the areas of health, education, housing, employment and economic development, and police-community relations, with WOPC having 51 percent of the members of each committee. Finally, it was agreed that both the city manager and the WOPC would be able to veto Model Cities proposals for bloc grants which originated with the agency and city council.

Soon after extracting these concessions from the city, WOPC raised the question of whether it would have veto power over all monies spent in the Model Cities area, not just over those bloc grants initiated by the city. This broader veto, which the OEO and U.S. Department of Labor seemed ready to grant,[25] would have given the West Oakland group control over the downtown Civic Center project and the port lands, all of which were included in the original Model Cities area, as well as several millions of dollars going to the Oakland police force. The WOPC argued that Model Cities was intended not only to initiate new money programs, but to coordinate existing spending programs in the Model Cities area, and that the provision of double veto should apply to all money. The city objected and, in the agency's revised Model Cities plan of April 1968, the downtown project and all port lands were deleted from the program area.

This action by the agency outraged WOPC, which felt that the $23 million slated for port development would now be used without reference to the needs of the West Oakland area. But it has not been able to reverse the agency decision. Instead, WOPC has moved toward direct negotiation with the city school board, port authority, county welfare department, and all local agencies spending money in the program area. Given its organized strength this is a significant tactic.

The WOPC, which has stated that "the ultimate aim of WOPC is to establish a city within a city" and which called its first president, Ralph Williams, the Mayor of West Oakland, has created a political base large enough to extract significant concessions from the bureaucracies. It has been militant: few agency employees appreciate its constant sharp criticism or its ability to involve the masses in successfully influencing the policy process. WOPC's rhetoric of political struggle and territorial independence (self-government) for the West Oakland residents has forced Downtown to heed the wishes of the neighborhood. Thus WOPC represents a radical pluralism: it has forced itself into the policy process previously monopolized by the city government. Compared to the purely administrative decentralization of OCNA, or the pluralism of powerful public and private agencies who designed the renewal program, WOPC represents real decentralization of power and a voice for the poor.

NOTES

1. "Community Redevelopment Law", *Statutes of the State of California,* 1945, chap. 1326.
2. Oakland Redevelopment Agency, "City Center, Oakland, California," June 24, 1966, p. 12.
3. The information in this paragraph was supplied by a member of the redevelopment agency.
4. Oakland *Catholic Voice,* April 7, 1966, p. 10.
5. Loren Mowry, interview, March 9, 1966.
6. Oakland *Tribune,* November 13, 1969, p. 13. Regional administrators of the Model Cities program were recently given the legal authority to suspend certification of programs if citizen participation or relocation assistance provisions are not in accordance with HUD guidelines.
7. Much of the information of the redevelopment program from 1954 to 1957 comes from newspaper clippings of the Oakland *Tribune* maintained by the secretary of OCCUR.
8. *Final Report of the Clinton Parks Project* (no date), p. 8.
9. Oakland *Catholic Voice,* April 7, 1966, p. 9.
10. The paper did not refer to West Oakland as a ghetto because of a policy it then had. In 1966 a reporter for the paper, writing up an article in which he quoted a speaker who had used the phrase "Oakland ghetto," was surprised to find that his article appeared in print with the word "ghetto" removed.

Irritated by the cavalier treatment his article had received, and thinking the copy desk to blame, he wrote a note critical of the copy desk and pinned it to the newsroom bulletin board. About four hours later another note, this time from the copy desk, was pinned below the reporter's. In it the copy desk denied having deleted the word "ghetto" in this instance, but added: "... We WOULD have removed 'ghetto', too. We do it even in tape-set wire stories because we have been instructed that it is (this paper's) policy never to use 'ghetto.' There are no slums in Oakland; there are no ghettoes anywhere. Now you know." Source: Oakland *Montclarion,* June 15, 1966, p. 20. But around 1968 the *Tribune* changed its policy and now prints news about ghettoes in and out of Oakland.

11. Oakland Renewal Foundation, *Final Report,* 1960(?).
12. Department of Building and Housing, *Annual Report,* 1960, p. 20.
13. The figure of 1,900 demolitions in Oak Center appears in the Oakland Planning Commission report (701 Project), "Changes in the Housing Inventory, 1960-1970," last page. The figure of 2,749 was obtained by telephone from the agency's public information officer.
14. Oakland Redevelopment agency, *Oakland, A Demonstration City Report,* 1966 (hereafter referred to as *Report).*
15. An income of $3,000 was necessary to qualify for a Federal loan under terms of section 221D-3 of the Federal Housing Act in 1966, according to the *Report,* p. 25. Yet nearly 4 out of 10 families in the project area, about 40 percent, earn under $3,000, p. 4. Hence 40 percent of all families living in the area would be too poor, if homeowners, to receive Federal aid for rehabilitation and could be evicted.
16. *Report,* p. 18.
17. Ibid. p. 21.
18. Ibid., p. 28.
19. Oakland *Tribune,* February 18, 1966, p. 1.
20. See Martin Anderson, *The Federal Bulldozer,* New York: McGraw-Hill, 1967, p. 130.
21. For an analytic approach to "maximum participation," written when the idea of participation by the poor was in a relatively early stage, see Peter Maris and Martin Rein, *Dilemmas of Social Reform, Poverty and Community Action in the United States.* A critique-analysis is in Daniel Moynihan, *Maximum Feasible Misunderstanding, Community Action in the War on Poverty,* New York: Free Press, 1970. A general analysis of the issues and possibilities of community control is in Alan Altschuler, *Community Control: The Black Demand for Participation in Large American Cities,* New York: Pegasus, 1970. A general criticism of the "myth" of community control is by Stanley Aronowitz, "The Dialectics of Community Control," *Social Policy,* May-June 1970, pp. 47-51.
22. Throughout the 1960s one councilman, Howard Rilea, did consistently criticize the renewal agency for driving people out of their homes. He was

one of two city councilmen, out of a total of nine, who won election without *Tribune* endorsement since 1945.

23. John Dole, "Redevelopment in Oakland," seminar paper, University of California, Berkeley, Department of Urban Design, Spring 1966.
24. Judy May, "Two Model Cities: Political Development on the Local Level," paper delivered at the American Political Science Association meeting, September 1969, p. 22. See also Miss May's doctoral disertation in progress, on the poverty program and Model Cities program of Oakland, University of California, Berkeley (Department of Political Science).
25. Hans Spiegel and S. Mittenthal, *Neighborhood Power and Control: Implications for Urban Planning,* Columbia University School of Architecture, November 1966 (microfiche), chap. 4.
26. The departments of HEW and HUD were more evasive in their replies to WOPC questions. See Judy May, "Two Model Cities . . ." p. 46.

The City and Poverty:
National Policies

The next three chapters deal with the major programs operating in Alameda county that are designed to cope with the problems of poverty and joblessness. Here we note the national policy context within which the city's local programs have been shaped.

The problems of poverty, economic dependence, and joblessness are at least as old as the American econopolitical system itself. Small efforts to deal with them in the United States began with the New Deal programs of the 1930s, including small efforts to stimulate regional economic development (the TVA), comprehensive planning (National Resources Planning Board); government employment programs (WPA, CCC), and Social Security, to name only some. After World War II the Congress passed the Employment Act, which pledged government to maintain employment, but which did not pledge it to full employment.[1] Through the presidencies of Truman and Eisenhower (1948-1960), poverty and joblessness per se were the subjects of no important national legislation.

In the 1960s the Federal government began a new series of approaches to the problems of unemployment, including aids to private industry, the poverty program, and manpower training programs. At the start of the 1970s there is a national debate on Guaranteed Annual Income (GAI), negative income tax, and vouchers to school-children.[2] All of these approaches are partial; none is represented, even by its sponsors, as an end to poverty. And if, as was argued in Chapter Three, poverty is an inseparable part of the present economic system, we should not expect these reforms to be more than partial solutions.

The following chapters will deal with the policy-making process and output of these national programs as they affect Oakland, specifically in the following areas: who makes local policy and how Federal policies and grants manipulate the local power situation; who benefits from the economic largesse provided or stimulated by these programs; and the extent to which these programs actually have succeeded in making any *significant* progress towards eliminating the fact of economic dependency. From these considerations we should arrive at a clearer understanding of the ability or inability of the present American urban political system to deal with the poverty problem in the future.

NOTES

1. In any event such a policy, had it been enacted, would probably mean as little as the 1949 Housing Act which guaranted "a decent home in a suitable living environment for every American." The 1946 Employment Act declares only that Congress will use its resources to create, ". . . in a manner calculated to foster and promote free competitive enterprise and the general welfare, conditions under which there will be afforded useful employment opportunities, including self-employment, for those able, willing, and seeking to work, and to promote maximum employment, production, and purchasing power." U.S. Congress, Joint Economic Committee, *Employment Act of 1946, as Amended, with Related Laws and Rules of the Joint Economic Committee,* 89th Cong., 2d Sess., 1966, p. 1.

2. As proposed by the Welfare Rights Organization, the minimum GAI for a family of four should be $5,500 per annum; as proposed to Congress by President Nixon, $1,600. See "The Nixon Proposal for Major Public Welfare Revision," *Congressional Digest,* 49, pp. 161-192, June-July 1970. See also Sar Levitan, *Programs in Aid of the Poor for the Seventies;* and George Rohrlich, ed., *Social Economics for the 1970s, Programs for Social Security, Health, and Manpower,* New York: Dunellen, 1970.

CHAPTER SIX

The Politics
of Poverty, I:
Control of the County
Welfare Department

CONTROLLING INFLUENCES OVER WELFARE POLICY

With the passage of the Federal Social Security Act in 1953, and the entry of the State of California into welfare grants to counties in 1932, the structure of power over Alameda welfare has been statewide and national in scope, directed at the national level by the Federal Department of Health, Education, and Welfare. This department provides a flexible set of rules for state and local welfare administrators and legislators, while in California the state legislature sets the specific level of aid to be granted welfare recipients in almost all programs.

Federal and state levels of authority together supply the vast bulk of welfare money spent in any county in California; local contributors provide a distinctly minor share. In 1965, of the total of $65 million paid out by Alameda County in welfare expenditures, only $11 million, or 17.3 percent, was raised by local taxes, the rest coming from the state ($23 million, 36.7 percent of the county welfare bill) or Federal government ($29 million, 46.23 percent).[1] This apparently gives both the state and Federal governments considerable leverage with which to make welfare policy at the county level. In Alameda, as in other California counties and much of the nation, the only program which the county wholly supports from local taxation, and in which the county itself sets the level of grants for each aid category is General Assistance. Thus control of the national or statewide political administrations has an important effect on the function of all welfare programs in California as in other states.

At the county level welfare policy is made by the board of supervisors and the top two or three administrators in the welfare department. In Alameda, this means that the majority of policy-makers are, and have been, hostile towards proposals for substantial increases in payments to welfare recipients. In 1968, three of the county's five supervisors were Democrats. One of these and both Republicans were "economy minded"; another, chairman of the supervisors subcommittee on welfare matters, campaigned for election in 1966 on a "cut welfare" platform. (This concern for economy did not prevent the supervisors from raising their own salary by $3,000 in 1970, to $17,500 for each supervisor). Until recently, supervisors in Alameda County have been conservative Republican, while the statewide county supervisors' association is a powerful voice for minimizing welfare levels at both county and state levels of government.

Policy and appointments at the board of supervisors have, until very recently, been dominated by the Republican party, itself the party of the Oakland *Tribune,* small and large business, and conservative voters. Before the welfare program, the Alameda County Charities Commission, organized in 1932 to coordinate public and private welfare activity, was almost wholly business-directed. Meeting in the Central National Bank building at Fourteenth Street and Broadway, the commission was chaired by A. J. Mount, then President of the Central National Bank. At an early meeting of the commission it was decided that the best way to relieve the heavy increase in welfare payments caused by the Depression would be through the passage of a public bond issue, and that an advisory committee of businessmen should be called to confer with the commission on the subject. Three such businessmen met, along with several members of the board of supervisors, and approved the bond issue.[2] Two weeks later the board of supervisors approved the issue. The city chamber of commerce was put in charge of the entire campaign for passage of the bonds at the next election; and the then District Attorney, later United States Supreme Court Justice, Earl Warren, together with members of the commission and a Supervisor, worked up a fact sheet supporting passage of the measure. The bonds, $1.5 million at 5 percent premium, were passed by the voters at the next election. Here was a policy initiated by business-men and carried out by a business-political combination.

The *Tribune* has always played an important role in welfare. In 1933 the paper's publisher, Joseph Knowland, was appointed to the Alameda County Emergency Relief Committee which appropriated relief throughout the duration of the Depression. As one longtime employee of the department put it, "The *Tribune* had a hand in setting up the Committee." Along with Knowland on the ERC was a furniture store owner, the president of a small printing company, and the wife of an official of the county public utility district. Since the 1930s the welfare department itself has been directed by several civil servants who have risen through the ranks of the department; yet the policies of the department have, until lately, changed very slowly, and the *Tribune* in its editorial column has always registered satisfaction with appointments to top positions in the department. Joseph Knowland was an early chairman of the Welfare Commission of Alameda County and remained a member until well after 1960.

Since the demise of its Hearst rival, the *Post-Inquirer,* in 1953,[3] the *Tribune* has been the city's only big newspaper, and it is this monopoly which gives the paper its great and continuing power over county welfare policy formation. The paper editorializes as often as a dozen times a year on welfare policy, and prints an annual double column lead story during the preparation of the county budget, heralding the rise in expenditures anticipated for the coming year and concentrating on the absolute size and annual increase of the welfare budget. In 1967, for example, the article began under a headline which read:

Welfare Bill to
Increase County Tax

and then continued: "Mounting health and welfare costs will force a 'significant' increase in Alameda County property taxes for 1967-1968." The editorial column in 1967 attacked proposed increases in Federal Social Security allotments, while in 1965 an editorial urged an amendment to the state constitution which would have obligated the state to shoulder a greater share of county welfare costs, a measure which the Alameda County Taxpayers Association and Alameda County Industries, Inc., also endorsed.[4]

The result of these news and editorial policies is to foster an antiwelfare climate of opinion in the county, to turn the overburdened small property owner against the poor and unemployed, and to ease the job of the supervisors in holding the line on welfare. It has likewise made extremely difficult any public criticism of the methods of welfare administration of the department. And it has made it possible, in the words of an official state report, for the department's top administration to form a "tight little group" within an "ingrown organization."[5]

Welfare Policies in Alameda County

The Alameda County Welfare Department gives very small amounts of aid. Housing grants for AFDC cases in 1968, as set by the state, went no higher than $43 a month for a single person, and no higher than $67 for a family of eight. The impossibility of finding adequate accommodations for a large family on such a budget is obvious, and frequently recipients must take money out of food and clothing budgets to pay the rent. Because the Federal government will not participate beyond $300 for this same eight-person family, the state and county limit their own contributions so as to get the maximum contribution from Washington. As Deputy Director Laurence Rainey has stated, "The only real answer for a woman with such a large family is to have her own income."[6] In short, welfare is not enough to live on, as those who administer it are aware.

This shortage is illustrated in another program, General Assistance, for which the state sets the payments schedule and the county provides the money. In GA as of December 1967, the basic food allotment for a single man on the program was $27.40 per month, about 33 cents per meal per day. The maximum which a single man could receive for housing on GA that year was $35 a month, an amount which confined him to a cheap hotel. Incidental needs—for all items outside the basic food, clothing, and housing allotments for the month—amounted to $4.00, an amount supposed to cover all expenses for furniture, transportation, entertainment, laundry, etc. The special clothing allowance for people on GA was $15 maximum over six months time, but could be received only if a separate itemized request was made. Food, rent, and supplies for a single man amounted to a total of $66.40 per month, or $796.80 annually, less than half the amount of income which the Federal government defined as the poverty level.

The agency, until recently, has been severe in its criteria for putting someone on aid, and quick to drop recipients. A routine review by the state of Alameda's welfare administration in 1965 criticized the county's "overly rigid" requirements of verification of residence and commented:

> People are usually denied assistance unless consistent records are available to prove residence, though no contradictory evidence exists. Farm laborers who make Alameda County their home but need to follow the crops find it particularly difficult to prove residence. . . . Single able-bodied men are denied assistance on the erroneous assumption that some work is always available for them.[7]

A special review by the state in the summer of 1964, when the county was denying welfare to all AFDC cases and sending them to farm labor, found that 49 individuals whom the county referred to farm labor work had been denied their welfare under procedures contrary to the welfare and institutions code of the state and state welfare guidelines (see ahead, p. 137). The Welfare Rights Organization estimates that it has helped well over 1,000 recipients regain welfare checks to which they were legally entitled; and that over 40 percent of the cases appealed by individuals before the WRO came into existence were decided in favor of the recipient.

Social workers for the department also have had complaints. The county has had a very large turnover in welfare workers, going as high as 38 percent in a single month.[8] A local organizer for the social workers union who was also a social worker put it as follows:

> My complaint is that as a social worker a guy gets hung up in these screwy rules. In AFDC, every case must have deprivation status. That means, for the child to qualify for welfare aid his father must be dead, or unemployed, or sick—totally without income. This means a guy who is employed, but $100 below the legal schedule for aid, can't get any help. Yet if he were the stepfather of one child in the house he could get help.[9]

As further illustration this organizer gave his own experience as a social worker:

> I was working with a poor Mexican family. The father had ten kids, and when he finally got a job and got off welfare he was earning less

for his family than when he was on welfare. This hits you right in the gut.

These experiences led him to the conclusion that "the working conditions on the job don't permit social workers to do social work," and brought him, and many like him, into the union.

ANTITHESIS: DEVELOPMENT OF A WELFARE OPPOSITION

The results of these conditions have been the formation of two opposition groups which have attacked the welfare policies of the department and the board of supervisors. The Welfare Rights Organization, a formation of welfare workers and political radicals, began its work in the county in 1964 to help welfare recipients who had been cut off welfare regain their allowances; the Social Services Union (SSU) Local 535, an AFL-CIO local for county welfare employees, began in Alameda County one year later to organize around the question of working conditions for welfare employees and around the whole range of policy questions which previously the director and county supervisors had decided themselves, including such questions as physical arrangements inside the welfare department building, amounts of money granted recipients in different programs, number of regional offices of the department, and the over-all administration of county programs.

The conflicts which these organizations have had with the welfare bureaucracy to change allotments in the interest of the poor recipients and to improve the conditions of work for welfare employees illustrates the problems of change, the obstacles to creating a pluralism in which the poor and employed have any *direct* influence over policy, and the powerlessness of the unorganized. The following are examples.

The SSU has organized like any industrial union, going on strike in Sacramento in early 1967 and demanding recognition and collective bargaining procedures. In early 1968, through a campaign of leaflets and public meetings, the Union pressured the county to raise the food allowance from $29 to $35 a month—along with other increases which raised the total county General Assistance bill by $168,097, or almost 25 percent. To gain this small increase required almost a year's intense effort, and two citywide public forums; eight months of this period had elapsed before the union could win a simple hearing before the board of supervisors.

The WRO's experience[10] also shows the efforts necessary to register change. In 1964, the state eliminated the imported braceros (farm-pickers) from Mexico, and passed a bill which required welfare recipients to accept any job offered or lose their welfare payments. The press speculated at the time that this law was passed to provide cheap farm labor, thereby compensating the growers for the absence of braceros. In May of that year Alameda County sent a letter to about 350 welfare recipients informing them of the need for farm laborers, asking them to contact the farm labor office, and warning them that "failure to do so may jeopardize your eligibility" for welfare payments. WRO charged that the county was yielding to pressure from the county's strawberry farmers to supply cheap labor, and further that the actual wages paid to those who were sent out to the strawberry fields were piecework rates amounting to only 60 cents an hour.[11] In the meantime the county refused welfare aid to many, claiming that there was work available in the fields and any who did not take it could not, under state law, receive welfare.

WRO replied that unemployed urban workers should not be forced to take piecework jobs at stoop labor as a condition of getting welfare, and pointed out that taking such labor made it impossible for skilled laborers to find work in their own field when it became available. The organization also charged that people who were not physically fit were being sent out to the fields after only the most perfunctory medical examinations.

In response to these charges the welfare department was criticized in a resolution read on the floor of the county labor council; the California state welfare agency investigated 49 cases of recipients who had been denied welfare and sent to farm labor, finding that state law and administrative regulations had been violated in each of the 49 cases,[12] and that the physically unfit had been sent to farm labor, including one worker with a bleeding colon. The state agency then ordered the county to reinstate all 49 recipients and to accept the unemployed back on the welfare rolls. None of these steps would have been taken if there had been no organization to articulate the demands of welfare recipients; the unorganized influence of recipients would have amounted to unrestricted referral to low-paying stoop labor jobs.

Even with the protest mounted by WRO the county continued the same practices, accepting the unemployed's applications for welfare but still demanding that they take farm labor or lose their application. By July the county was again threatening to cut more from the welfare rolls. In September, with no change in sight, and with the county refusing to meet for negotiations, WRO held a large sit-in at the county welfare building, the first welfare sit-in in the country.

The result was that the county locked the demonstrators into the building, telegrams of support for the demonstrators came from many parts of the country, and the county supervisors, feeling the pressure, ordered the welfare department to negotiate with WRO. And as a result of these negotiations, the county agreed to improve its medical examination procedures in farm labor referrals and to improve other aspects of welfare administration. But the questions of referring unemployed sheet metal workers to strawberry picking, and underpayment of farm pickers, remained; WRO in September threatened a second sit-in in the San Francisco offices of the California state welfare department, and in the face of this threatened action, the state director of welfare issued Bulletin No. 644, which redefined farm labor as "part time," thereby allowing those who picked in the fields to continue to receive welfare aid.[13]

Conclusion: Power of Welfare v. Power of Employees and Poor

The gains made by WRO and SSU are more than the above illustrations would indicate. In addition to increasing the amounts paid for General Welfare and improving farm labor referrals, other changes have been made: through a suit by Legal Aid, the one-year waiting requirement has been abolished so that those whose income is low enough can go on welfare immediately upon moving into the county. Stolen or lost checks are now repaid within two weeks instead of four, and no one is compelled to go out to farm labor during the non-summer months. Given these changes it is appropriate at this point to ask, whether a real pluralism in decision making has developed on questions of welfare.

This question leads to a central question of this book, namely, how shall we define pluralism? If it is defined as "a lot of people and agencies who have some influence," then of course pluralism exists; the problem with that definition, which is a thumbnail description of what the school of pluralism offers us as the substance of pluralism,[14] is that pluralism of that sort existed *before* WRO and SSU appeared on the scene. While the *Tribune* played a constant and important role in policy making, still a multiplicity of actors existed, from the Federal government down to the director of the county department.

But if pluralism is defined not simply as the number of individuals participating in decisions, but as the extent to which various social classes are represented by the political system; and if reform pluralism is defined as that situation in which the poor and laboring classes are able to achieve economic and working condition gains through political organization and movement, then the answer to the question, "Is there pluralism in county welfare decisions?" is not so simple. In 1971, after several years of organization and struggle, the gains seem very small.[15] All welfare recipients are still sent automatically to farm labor in the summer, and their welfare is suspended; regular caseworkers carry caseloads of 80 recipients, far too many to do any significant rehabilitative work. The SWU, four years after its creation, and with over 6,500 statewide members, still is not recognized as bargaining agent for county welfare employees[16] whose pay increases have averaged 5 percent in recent years. And, strikingly, in 1970 the state department of welfare issued new AFDC regulations which will result in raising payments in housing costs, but lowering payments in other categories so that, according to an SSU estimate, payments will actually be cut for 40 percent of the state's welfare recipients.[17] Thus the actual direct power of the welfare poor, measured as their ability to improve their economic status through legislative reform, is only a little greater today than in the early 1960s.

NOTES

1. Alameda County Board of Supervisors, *Alameda County, The Changing Scene,* November 1965, p. 25.
2. Welfare Commission of Alameda County, *Minutes,* October 13, 1932.
3. The *Post-Inquirer's* death remains something of a mystery. It shut its doors suddenly, without prior indication of financial diffculties, and never passed along its lists of subscribers to other Bay Area papers.
4. Oakland *Tribune,* April 29, 1965. In fact the state has been increasing its share of welfare expenses; in 1965 Alameda County paid only 17.3 percent of the total county welfare bill.
5. State Department of Social Welfare, "Administrative Review of Alameda County Welfare Department," July 1965, p. iii.

6. Interview, December 1967.

7. State Department of Social Welfare, op. cit., Appendix D.

8. Irving Kermish and Frank Kushin, *An Examination of Variables Influencing Social Work Staff Turnover at a Public Welfare Agency,* Submitted to the State Department of Social Welfare, December 1967, pp. 10 and 79.

9. Randy Serrurier, interview, January 1968.

10. The author wishes to thank Mrs. Virginia Proctor for providing basic facts on welfare and WRO in Alameda County.

11. San Francisco *Examiner,* October 6, 1964.

12. State Department of Social Welfare, op. cit., p. 2.

13. State of California, Department of Social Welfare, *Department Bulletin No.* 644 (AFDC) (Revised), September 8, 1965.

14. See, for instance, R. N. Polsby, *Community Power and Political Theory,* New Haven: Yale University, 1963, chap. 6.

15. The author wishes to thank Mr. John Bowers for several of the facts used in this paragraph.

16. Indeed the SWU's moderate rival, the Alameda County Employees Association, is not recognized either; the county had recognized no bargaining agent for county employees as of December 1970.

17. Bill Caddy, "Welfare Cuts, Percentages versus Reality," Richmond, California *Freedom News,* December 1970, p. 11.

CHAPTER SEVEN

The Politics of Poverty, II:
Control and Content of Antipoverty Programs, 1943-1970

THE LEAN YEARS, 1943-1970

Under the pressure of widescale unemployment during the decade of the Great Depression, the California legislature created the California State Planning Board,[1] a statewide version of the National Resources Planning Board having the same general features and mission. Both the state and national agencies included as their raison d'être a coordinated attack via central planning bodies on the interrelated problems of resource development. In the 1940s, opposed by a political coalition which included big business and anti-New Deal congressional Republicans, who both preferred not to have a national agency with such a potential for independent power, the NRPB was abolished, and so was its California analogue.[2]

In place of the state planning board the California legislature created a Reconstruction and Reemployment Commission, with a broad planning mandate which included the prevention of unemployment. Yet as one observer noted in regard to the new agency, "it was obvious that the legislature intended it to stress industrial expansion and the planning of public works."[3] A San Francisco businessman was appointed to direct the new agency. According to Mel Scott, "The commission sought regional cooperation, but of the sort that chambers of commerce and other business groups had sought from time to time in the past fifteen years."[4]

The new commission held hearings in the chambers of the Oakland City Council on August 23 and 24, 1944. Of the 37 men who spoke at this meeting, 8 were chamber of commerce or trade association officials, 5 were corporation officials of private business corporations, 4 were elected officials of state or county government, 4 were representatives of local or county governments, 3 were officers of private planning or development associations, and 5 of unidentified affiliation, but made generally favorable comments to the industrial approach to postwar planning. Thus almost one-third of the identified speakers at this meeting were clearly from business or business-oriented organizations, and constituted the biggest single interest group in attendance. The primary interest of members of the commission was industrial development, with government supplying the roads and other necessary infrastructure for such development. Jobs and housing for working people were not priority objectives. As one member of the commission summed it up: "Industry can do the job—but government must step into the gaps."[5]

From this meeting came an important, Bay Area-wide group, the San Francisco Bay Region Council (now called the San Francisco Bay Area Council, or BAC) whose function would be to deal with development problems in the Bay Area, including transportation, schools, bay pollution, jobs, and industrial development. The council was intended to stress joint efforts by Bay Area governments and business firms. But control of the council has rested overwhelmingly with business. Frank N. Belgrano, Jr., President of the Central Bank of Oakland, was named Chairman of the first Council[6] and R. E. Fisher, Vice-President of the Pacific Gas and Electric Company, was selected as Vice-Chairman. Mr. Fisher's list of the six most urgent needs of the Bay Area included, first, promotion of foreign trade and, second, expenditures to advertise the Bay region as a good place to invest. The list also included such items as the need for increased aviation facilities, improved highway and rail transportation, bridge and highway development, and public works. The list did not mention jobs or unemployment. Thus regional planning after World War II dealt with the priorities set by the area's industrial-financial elite, who showed no major concern for poverty or poverty-related problems, but who did show an enormous interest in directing government activities to increase the moneymaking abilities of their corporations.

In 1964 the Bay Area Council's governing bodies continued to represent a cross section of the important institutions in the Bay region, yet the greatest percentage came from business firms and associations, as is shown in Table 7-1.

The extent of control over BAC by private corporations is indicated by the social backgrounds of its executive officers and several governing bodies. The Chairman of BAC in 1965 was S. C. Biese, who in private life was Chairman of the Executive Committee of the Bank of America, the Bank's highest position. Other officers included Cyril Magnin, president of Joseph Magnin, a major San Francisco department store. Every one of its leading officers was a top executive of a major local or national corporation; the composition of its board of governors shows a clear hegemony of business representatives (see Table 7-1); and its other two governing bodies are even more completely dominated by business.[7] There can be little doubt which private influences have directed the BAC's policies in its extensive areas of concern. The continuing breadth of its mandate is indicated by its own literature: "The Council

TABLE 7-1   Organizational affiliation of members, Board of Governors, San Francisco Bay Area Council, 1964-65

Business firms, associations	91
National, state firms	31
Regional firms	47
Business associations	13
Government officials (regional and local)	23
elected	19
appointed	4
Communications	14
Newspapers	10
TV, radio	4
Colleges, universities	7
Labor Organizations	8
Private associations	4
Unidentified	1
Total	148

Source: Bay Area Council, *Bay Area Council, 1964-1965 Officers*, San Francisco, 1964(?).

is concerned with regional matters including transportation, land use planning, air and water pollution control, recreational development, and economic transportation."

The significance of the control and program of the Bay Area Council derives from the fact that, between its creation in 1945 and the formation of the Association of Bay Area Governments (ABAG)* in 1961, the Council was itself preeminent in the field of comprehensive regional planning and was influential in creating two other major Bay Area planning groups, the Bay Area Planning Directors' Committee and the Bay Area Congress of Citizens Organizations. Thus throughout the postwar years one, if not *the* most influential, of the regional planning associations, was the creature of private business. Today the Association of Bay Area Governments plays at least as great a regional role as BAC.[8]

Within Oakland immediately after the war a Postwar Planning Committee was appointed by the Mayor, Dr. John F. Slavich. Dr. Slavich, himself a civic activist, appointed a committee which included a who's who of local business leaders, along with a sampling of trade unionists, political leaders, and members of the public. The executive committee of the new group included P.D. Richardson of the Bank of America, Mayor Slavich, City Manager Charles Schwanenberg, two AFL officials, the Manager and two staff members of the Oakland Chamber of Commerce, and the President of William Cavalier Company. The general committee included executives from General Electric, American Trust, the Central Bank of Oakland, and the Oakland *Tribune,* plus all the members of the Oakland City Council. Of the general committee's 40 members, 26 were officials of local or statewide businesses.[9]

At the end of its period of study the committee made 16 recommendations, of which the key recommendation was for an omnibus bond issue to promote six separate areas of civic development. The city departments, asked to submit a list of needed projects, submitted a request for 316 projects at a total cost of just over $181 million. City Manager Schwanenberg stated, in supporting the two $15 million bond proposals which were finally agreed upon, that the new bonds made

*ABAG, an association of Bay Area governments, now has a comprehensive regional planning function and considerable influence and is clearly staffed by governmental, as opposed to business, representatives.

possible a building program which "includes many improvements deferred as much as twenty years."[10]

On May 8, 1945, the city's voters approved the first bond issue for $15 million dollars, but in October of the same year the second $15 million issue, for school facilities, was defeated.* In a city which had a bonded indebtedness of almost zero, and hence was in a sound financial position; and which had requests from its own department heads for over $180 million, the decision to ask the voters for no more than $30 million was a decision for severe fiscal stringency. The first bond issue provided minimal improvements for libraries, streets, sewers, playgrounds, and swimming pools. The largest item on the bond proposal, for $2 million dollars, was ear marked for a new Hall of Justice to house municipal courts and the city police department. As a consequence of these small bond revenues, the city's schools, streets, branch libraries and other facilities continued without expansion or renovation, a condition which contributed to the need for some kind of urban renewal and redevelopment in the 1960s.

Despite the objectives stated by the committee at the outset of its activities, none of the recommendations contained in its final report dealt with the Oakland housing shortage, nor did they point to any substantial sources of money to combat poverty, beyond the money allocated for jobs by the street and sewers bond issue. The rationale of the committee's work was given in the report, as follows:

> Immediate and postwar civic improvements will have a far-reaching effect on Oakland's industrial development. Eastern concerns are more likely to locate their plants in Oakland, knowing that the City of Oakland is willing to provide the facilities required by industry. With the expansion of our highways and freeways and other planned civic improvements, Oakland is purchasing in advance the industrial expansion and growth which will make this the leading center of the New Industrial West.[11]

In short, civic improvements were to be just large enough to attract industry. Thus the city's businessmen and officials directly controlled a major public activity in accordance with corporate priorities. The first

---

*The Committee never explained why the two bond issues were separated; had both been voted for in the election of May 8 and given strong support by the city's leadership, both might very well have passed.

real attempt by the city to deal specifically with social problems was still a dozen years in the future.

The Interagency Project

In 1961–1962 the city organized the Oakland Interagency Project (OIP), with assistance from the Ford Foundation as a part of the foundation's Gray Areas program. OIP created a local council of state and city agencies primarily concerned with high school youth. Its formation was stimulated by a student-led disturbance in the Castlemont High School in the east-central section of the city, and by the decline in income status of residents of the Castlemont area. To control future outbreaks, and to reassure middle-income tenants of the desireability of staying in the area, top officials from police, welfare, school, and probation departments met to exchange information on specific students and to identify problem situations in advance. Thus social control was the primary initial purpose of OIP, and while the program later developed counseling and remedial reading projects in Castlemont and about half of Castelmont's feeder schools, the latter programs were so small that they accomplished little.[12]

The city's economic elite played a central role in creating and sustaining the program. In addition to the operating council of government officials, the OIP had an advisory committee of 15 members, 9 of whom were local businessmen and corporate executives, including the publisher of the *Tribune*. The advisory committee signed the first funding proposal of the project; it maintained the legal power to review programs in the first years; and its advisory committee helped provide community support which, in the opinion of the city manager, was necessary for the program to function. Thus the city manager has written:

> At a breakfast meeting at the Kaiser building we explained to a representative group of community leaders the kind of program that was needed and requested their help in financing the application. On hearing the objectives of the proposed project, Senator William F. Knowland was the first to volunteer $1,000. Equal amounts were contributed by Edgar Kaiser and the Oakland Council of Social Planning. Edgar Buttner, the President Of the Oakland Chamber of

Commerce, volunteered that organization's assistance in handling all funds and disbursements.

Later in the same article the city manager writes: "Without this political and community leadership it would have been impossible to move ahead."[13]

THE WAR ON POVERTY

Passage of the Equal Opportunity Act (EOA) by the United States Congress in 1964 created a new situation in Oakland as in other American cities. Now, for the first time since the New Deal, the question of poverty was to be attacked explicitly and not as a part of a juvenile control program or as a by-product of industrial development. The act called the poor onto the political stage as decision makers by requiring "maximum feasible participation of the residents of the areas and the members of the groups to be served" by the program. Thus the program was doubly new, new in its explicit concern for poverty and in its involvement of the poor.

Yet the OEO did not offer any great political authority to the poor, and since it developed at the same time as the riots in Watts, Cleveland, Newark, and dozens of other cities, we must ask whether this program was tokenism or real reform, a concession to cool down the growing anger in the black ghettoes in hundreds of cities or a pattern for future development.[14] The Oakland experience is part and parcel of OEO's national performance. Nothing tells us more about the intent and scope of the program than its formative period in the city, and we begin with that period.

In Oakland the mayor simply designated the business-dominated OIP Advisory Committee as the local community action agency with top control over the program; the committee was renamed the Oakland Economic Development Council (OEDC), and shortly the mayor added one representative from CORE, one from the NAACP, and one from the Mexican American Political Association. One of these three representatives of minorities was a small businessman and another a lawyer; the third had experience as a neighborhood organizer.

The EOA called for the creation of resident neighborhood councils in designated poverty areas. In Oakland the mayor called a meeting of the OEDC in December 1964, before advisory councils had been established. At that meeting the city manager proposed that the staff of OIP become the staff of OEDC; the OEDC approved this suggestion, renaming the staff the Department of Human Resources. The program director, who had already been nominated, presented a 12-point action program for the first nine months, at a cost of $810,181; the program and its nominated director were approved exactly as they had been proposed.[15] Thus the project's director, its administrative and staff structure, and the initial nine months of its program were all created by a business-dominated OEDC.

The OEDC soon created Target Area Advisory Committees (TAACs) in the four poorest sections of the city to serve as liaison between the poor and the OEDC. In effect this meant the target area committees had advisory authority and the power to initiate proposals, but not final authority over any program or over the community organizers paid by the downtown Council of Social Planning to gather residents' complaints about neighborhood conditions. And in Oakland the TAACs were not able to win what San Francisco's TAACs had almost from the start, the veto power over action proposals.[16]

The creation of the West Oakland Target Area Advisory Committee provides an illustration of how city hall created these committees and of the extent of their dependence. A conservative black priest in West Oakland was asked to set up the nucleus of the advisory committee for West Oakland in the spring of 1965. In March the first public meetings of the West Oakland Target Area Advisory Committee were held. Ensuing events are described by a onetime member of the West Oakland area TAAC:

> From this group (the nucleus) they went to the neighborhood. They selected Mrs. Love, an 'instant Negro' who owns property enough to make her comfortable, and who is chairman of the Oak Center Neighborhood Council of home *owners*. It is not a tenants association. She is Supervisor in the Welfare Department. (Note: From November 1966 until 1970 she served on the Board of Commissioners of the Oakland Redevelopment Agency.) She was selected to chair the meeting, and the OEDC there tried to sell the whole new program of fourteen proposals. Only about eight people were there. Then we (West Oakland Christian Parish) began to get more people

at the meetings, a number of us spoke against it. After that a group of about forty people met at our old parish and decided not to buy the program.[17]

The other target area advisory committees also felt that the program had been structured so as to keep the neighborhood committees from having any influence over important policy. Indeed the OEDC in its early months, even after the creation of target area committees, did not want these target areas to elect their own representatives to OEDC. And as events would later prove, OEDC itself was subservient to the city council. Hence clear elements of elitism are evident in the program's formative stages.

The Content of OEO's Oakland Program

During the two years that Ford Foundation supported the OIP, practically no money was spent specifically on community organizing. In the first three years of the OEDC, the poverty program spent only a small fraction of its total budget for this purpose. The over-all budget categories from 1964 to spring 1967 are shown in Table 7-2.

As Table 7-2 makes clear, service, education, and administration absorb 63.1 percent of all spending. The major item under jobs (just over $1.2 million for the Neighborhood Youth Corps) is an item which creates only temporary summer jobs. And only $304,998, about 6 percent of total expenditures, was devoted to organizing.[18]

TABLE 7-2 *Performance budget, Oakland's war on poverty, to Spring 1967*

1. Jobs	$1,886,354
2. Service	1,584,850
3. Education	1,154,408
4. Administration	1,004,624
5. Organization	304,998
Total	$5,935,234

Source: Compiled from figures in U.S. Senate Committee on Labor and Welfare, *Examination of the War on Poverty, Staff and Consultants Report, Vol VII* (Oakland), prepared for the Subcommittee on Employment, Manpower, and Poverty, 90th Cong., Washington: G.P.O., September 1967, pp. 2219-2220.

The application for OEO money submitted by the East Oakland Parish of community-involved priests offered a different approach to the poverty question. In the area of public housing, which the Federal program was ignoring, the parish application argued that:

> The same $800,000 which the Inter-Agency Project (OIP) is requesting and would spend primarily on middle-class salaries, could provide eighty to ninety decent safe and sanitary multi-bedroom apartments. . .About half of the $800,000 in such a project would go into salaries for low income people.[19]

The application stated that permanent job creation, an area in which the Federal program took very little interest, was an immediate problem; it called for massive tax subsidies to encourage business to locate in Oakland, and for a massive public works program. The Proposal demanded immediate use of Federal monies for rent subsidies; the immediate implementation of the Federal Food Stamp Program which was not operational in Alameda County until as late as the summer of 1968, four years after its creation by the Congress; and a limitation on the salaries of staff workers to $10,000 per year and of the director to $15,000 per year. The funds requested in the application are shown in Table 7-3.

The $1.5 million which the parish proposal requested for community organizing was still a half million less than San Francisco was spending for this activity.

TABLE 7-3 Poverty program as designed by the East Oakland Parish, 1965

New public housing	$ 3,500,000
Subsidies to industry	6,900,000
Temporary rent subsidy	1,000,000
Organizing the poor	1,500,000
Agency subsidy and stimulus	1,500,000
Staff and direction	500,000
Program evaluation	100,000
Total	$15,000,000

Source: East Oakland Parish, "Application for Funds under Title II-A of the Economic Opportunity Act of 1964," January 25, 1965.

The parish application clearly reflected a different set of priorities than did the OEDC's service and administration oriented program; the parish was convinced that their priorities lay closer to the real needs of the poor community. The Equal Opportunity Act provides that either public or private agencies can become the local CAA to guide the program, and the parish wanted to be so designated. Nevertheless the Federal OEO turned down their application and accepted the mayor's OEDC to wage war on the city's poverty.

Which program, OEDC's or EOP's, reflected the real priorities of the people of Oakland? Some evidence is supplied by a comprehensive survey of one-fiftieth of Oakland's total households, undertaken by the Survey Research Center of the University of California in the spring and summer of 1966. This survey divided the city into seven areas, four of which corresponded to the four target areas under the poverty program, and took an approximately equal number of households from each area. The survey deals broadly with definitions and incidence of poverty in the city. It also reports on questionnaires, administered to city residents, which measured residents' attitudes towards Oakland's war, and their opinions about it, including their estimate as to why Oakland wasn't doing a better job.

To get these answers the survey provided a set of 10 program choices. Respondents were asked to rank these choices according to which they thought were most needed in combatting poverty in the city. Answers were grouped by poverty or nonpoverty status for all respondents, and then for the target (poverty) areas and non-target areas. The results are shown in Table 7-4.

A comparison of Table 7-2 with Table 7-4 shows the clear difference in the priorities of the city's poor and nonpoor, on the one hand, and the priorities of the poverty program itself up to 1967. This difference contributed to neighborhood dissatisfaction with the program and laid a basis for the coming power struggle. It also supported the contention of the East Oakland Parish that the parish application reflected the real needs of the city's poor.

The Struggle for Control

The responses of target area residents to their TAACs were basically similar. A high initial attendance was followed by a rapid drop-off which resulted from several factors. First, the OEDC's administrative

TABLE 7-4 *Programs seen as really needed to help the poor in Oakland, by DHR poverty status and area: Oakland respondents, 1966*

| | Percentage of respondents describing program as really needed | | | | | | | | |
| | Oakland | | | Target areas | | | Non-target areas | | |
Programs	Tot.	Pov.	Non pov.	Tot.	Pov.	Non pov.	Tot.	Pov.	Non pov.
Have more job training programs	82	82	82	87	84	86	80	80	80
Bring more industries to Oakland	72	72	72	78	80	77	69	63	70
Have more government work projects	60	70	57	74	77	73	52	62	50
Build more low-rent housing	71	77	69	82	86	80	64	67	64
Increase welfare benefits	58	72	54	72	79	68	51	62	49
Make sure employers give minorities a fair chance at good jobs	74	76	74	81	81	81	71	69	71
Make sure unions accept minorities	73	75	72	79	79	78	69	69	69
Improve education for poor children	67	71	65	76	77	75	62	63	61
Have more preschool programs	59	61	59	68	68	68	54	52	54
Have more trained family counselors	54	56	53	60	62	60	50	50	50

Source: William L. Nicholls II, *Poverty and Poverty Programs in Oakland*, Berkeley: Survey Research Center, University of California, 1967, p. 101.

staff, titled the Department of Human Resources, carefully controlled TAAC suggestions for program content and discouraged popular initiative. As one West Oakland priest described it,

> When the people wanted to take direct action, like writing letters of complaint to city agencies, the DHR representative would always say 'Go through channels' which meant to go to the OEDC first. When money was allocated to build a housing code enforcement board of directors, the people said, 'Can the money be used for fixing up the houses?' He said 'No' for six months and then reversed himself.[20]

The lack of job orientation of the poverty program was a common complaint among the poor at a community forum in November 1965. A representative of the North Oakland TAAC summarized the view of many in attendance:

> What has really hurt us is that we do not get placement for the jobs. We (want to?) get them out of the poor state, given them some work to do. We had Mr.____ come to our meeting once, our regular club meeting; and when he mentioned the fact that there are not jobs for you, this killed the whole thing. . . . Ladies and gentlemen, to make the program a success, we're going to have to have some jobs for these people to help them get out of poverty. You give them some money, and they can do it themselves. How can you give them services? They need money to buy bread with for their children.[21]

Lacking any direct representation on the OEDC in the first months of their existence, or any authority over community organizers at work in their own neighborhoods, the advisory committees raised an early demand for membership on the OEDC. They called on the regional director of OEO, who aided them by warning the OEDC that as regional director he would discontinue Federal funds if target area representatives were not seated.[22] They raised constant criticism at OEDC meetings, including a walkout of one of the workshops planning the second year's program. All of this was carried in the local paper. Under these pressures the mayor and city council slowly relented, gradually enlarging the OEDC until it reached 40 persons, and granting a majority of seats to target area residents, in January of 1967.

The results of this new majority were quick in coming: in the same month, on a vote divided largely between the downtown government

and business representatives on the one hand and the flatlands representatives on the other, the new OEDC passed a proposal for a police
review board.

By voting for the review board the poor in Oakland achieved a small
first: a majority vote on an official ̀city agency contrary to the desires
of city officialdom. But by the same act the subordinate legal status of
OEDC, and the real limits which had existed on its authority the whole
time, came to the surface. The city council, which had control of all of
OEDC's requests for funds, vehemently refused the idea of a review
board and refused any funds for the project, thereby killing the idea for
over a year.

In the same year the original director of the Department of Human
Resources left the poverty program, raising the important question of
his successor. The target areas had already severely criticized his handling of their program proposals, and now wanted to appoint his
replacement, arguing that to use the normal method of appointment,
the city's civil service commission, would only result in a new director
as unsatisfactory as the old.[23] Unable to resolve the police review
board issue and the "succession crisis," the OEDC, now controlled by
the TAACs, split away from the city. In January 1968 it incorporated
itself as the independent Oakland Economic Development Council, Inc.
(OEDCI), directly under the Federal OEO and free of the direct
supervision of the local city council.[24]

Since 1968 the OEDCI has had a dramatic career. Its new director,
Percy Moore, is militant and began office with support of a boycott of
a local grocery store, called in retaliation against the police slaying of
Oakland Black Panther Bobby Hutton in 1968. When the OEDCI
attempted to hold a meeting in the fall of 1969 to discuss replacing
him, Moore's supporters surrounded the meeting place and, with chants
and shouts of support, prevented the attempted ouster from taking
place. He has clearly articulated the resentment of many of the black
population against the city's power holders and has proved himself capable both of holding his majority on the OEDCI and of maintaining
OEDCI's eligibility as the Community Action Agency in Oakland.[25]

A major part of Moore's success is attributable to the existence of
the Oakland Black Caucus, an organization of black organizations
whose leaders include members of the NAACP, CORE, the Urban
League, neighborhood groups, and Moore himself, and who have been

militant in their defense of the black community.[26] The caucus provided a black base of support for the election of Ronald Dellums as Congressman from the (Berkeley-Oakland) 7th Congressional District in 1970; several of its members, now on the OEDCI, have run for city office and have a good chance of winning election as councilman or, possibly, mayor. Thus the poverty program has resulted in building a power base for the poor in the city, something they have never had before; and it has resulted in formation of the West Oakland Planning Committee, a militant group capable of raising an effective voice for the poor in the Model Cities program (see Chapter Five, pp. 123-125).

Because creation of a police review board requires consent of the city council, OEDCI under Mr. Moore has been unable to create such a body; but the TAACs, supported by the caucus, have maintained a tenuous control over OEDCI and administered the program effectively.

Yet the program is also a token effort. The war on poverty has hardly fought even a preliminary skirmish, if poverty, and not city hall, is defined as the enemy. To raise the incomes of Oakland's 9,932 families living in extreme deprivation in 1959 to the above-deprivation level for 1965 ($6,000) would cost about $49.6 million annually. To raise the city's 24,151 poverty level families to the $6,000 level would cost $96.6 million annually; to raise its 45,266 deprivation level families to $6,000 would cost another $135 million, or a total of $281.2 million annually in income transfer payments. Those are the dimensions of poverty, measured in terms of income. In this light, the under $25 million that the poverty program has spent since its inception in 1964 through 1970 constitutes, in fact, a token amount. While the OEO never promised to make all men equal, and while it has used its money effectively in many cases, perhaps its greatest achievement is to show the enormous distance as yet untravelled by any antipoverty program. OEO is a long way ahead of the thinking of the Postwar Planning Committee, and far short of any real solutions.

The Poverty Program and its Critics

There have been several kinds of criticism of the war on poverty. Daniel Moynihan has written much and suggested, indirectly, that the national program suffered in part because the poor were not ready for the degree of self-government which the program, especially the community action phase, afforded:

It may be that the poor are never 'ready' to assume power in an advanced society: the exercise of power in an effective manner is an ability acquired through apprenticeship and seasoning. Thrust on an individual or group, the results are often painful to observe . . . [27]

The distaste of Mr. Moynihan for the rough-and-tumble, sometimes bitter, politics of the program and the attacks by the poor on Sargent Shriver, onetime head of OEO, represents a liberal's unwillingness to let the poor do for themselves. One could argue with force that the TAACs provided, in Oakland and elsewhere, the very "apprenticeship and seasoning" that Mr. Moynihan argues should be a *prerequisite* to political participation. If an observer suggests a prerequisite he should at least be willing to stand by his own recommendation.

The political left and liberal writers have raised a more serious set of criticisms. They have argued that the program did not provide enough power for the poor, that it went halfway, that it took radical organizers off the street and into "safe" administrative jobs, that it never had the money to provide more than token programs and failed to answer the main need of the poor, an adequate income.[28] In Oakland, all of these criticisms are almost entirely borne out. In one respect, however, the criticism does not fit. The black activists in OEDC have shown a toughness and an ability to stay independent of mayoral cooptation; their attacks on what they describe as the ruling class of the city remain an important source of uncoopted criticism of the city's power elite.

CONCLUSION: WHO RULED THE POVERTY PROGRAMS?

The overall scorecard of power over the city's poverty and job programs is given in Table 7-5.

The first column, initiator, refers to the person or agency which planned the program or called the first meetings of any program. The second column, direct executive control, refers to the highest levels of authority over the program at the urban level. The OIP, which had both a powerful advisory committee primarily composed of businessmen and an administrative leadership of operating department heads is scored in both business and government categories.

The third column, priorities, refers either to who sets the priorities, promoted by the program or *whom* these programs were *primarily*

TABLE 7-5   Political influence in poverty-related programs in Oakland, 1944-1971

Agencies	Categories of power and benefits																			
	Initiator					Direct executive control					Priorities					Benefits to social class				
	G*	B	M	L	P	G	B	M	L	P	G	B	M	L	P	G	B	M	L	P
Reconstruction and Reemployment Commission (RRC)		▓				▓					▓					◺	▓		▓	▓
Bau Area Council (BAC)†						▓	X									◺	▓		▓	▓
Postwar Planning Committee (PPC)	▓	▓				▓	X				▓	X				◺	▓		▓	▓
Oakland Interagency Project (OIP)	▓					▓	X				▓					◺				
Poverty Program (OEDC) before 1968	▓	▓				▓	X				▓	X				◺				
Poverty Program (OEDC) after 1968											▓	X			▓	◺			▓	▓

X refers to economic activists (Kaiser, *Tribune*)

†no data on initiator

*Letters on this row stand for: government, business, middle class, organized labor, and poor.

intended to benefit. Thus the Bay Area Council, with its emphasis on industrial development and opposition to strong planning controls, serves directly the priorities of the Bay Area industrial hierarchy, and only indirectly the interest of the middle class, which benefits from stronger planning controls. Hence the middle class is not scored. Because the needs of the poor, including housing and job creation, have never been high on BAC agenda, the poor are not scored. The case of the Postwar Planning Committee is similar. The PPC provided money for sewers, streets, and a central library that benefitted the city as a whole, but intended this minimal development not simply to insure the spiritual or cultural growth of the city, but largely as a means of guaranteeing Oakland's industrial growth, as PPC stated in its final report (see p. 145). Hence, while the city as a whole benefitted, the city's economic elite was intended as the *main*, or primary beneficiary. Government, whose estimate of need ran 10 times over the amount of PPC-approved bond issues, held a clearly inferior priority setting role.

The Interagency Project's (OIP) priorities are given a full scoring for government; the initial intention of the program, control of delinquent youth, was initiated in the first instance by government agencies, although it found an immediate response in the business community, which is also scored. Other sectors of the community are not scored, because the middle class city organizations and labor registered no comment on the program, while for the poor a program of increasing governmental control over their lives was contrary to their interests. The priorities column is based not only on whose priorities were realized, but on which groups were the *intended* beneficiaries. If *realization* were the *sole* criterion then in the case of OIP neither government nor business could be scored. The program simply did not produce results.

Because the group that directly controls a program and the group that sets and tries to realize its own priorities are likely to be one and the same group, columns two and three vary only slightly. For the Bay Area Council, the government is scored as having some priority (agenda) setting ability, although it is not scored as having top control, something which is strictly reserved for business. For the RRC, government officials maintained control over programs designed primarily to enhance the functioning of corporate enterprise. And, interestingly, the priorities of the poverty program were endorsed by the activist corporations, the *Tribune* and Kaiser companies, while the business community in general considered the program a waste of resources. Only in this program do we find the priorities of the politically active corporations differing from those of business generally; apparently when it comes to handling the poor, those corporations which play a permanent role in the governing of the city take a more realistic view of the utility of "token" programs than does the business community generally.

The poor are also scored as a priority setter in the OEDC. While this is strictly the case a word of caution is in order. These priorities are largely limited by Federal legislation and by the facts of political power in the city, and must filter upward through the state governor's office and national OEO. The priorities of OEDC do not include jobs, income, or housing to any great extent; hence the poor help set priorities only within a highly limited range of alternatives. By contrast the Reconstruction and Reemployment Commission, the Bay Area Council, and the Postwar Planning Committee all have been directly concerned with creating the necessary private and governmental assistance to fully realize the *first* priority of private industry: industrial development. There is a crucial difference between government activity which helps a group realize its first priority and activity which helps another group realize its second or third priority; the latter seems to characterize the poverty program.

The last column, benefits to social class, refers to the extent to which government programs have advanced the interest of various social classes in the city. Hence government itself, since it is not a social class, is not scored. A program which benefits a social class indirectly, or slightly, or which meets only secondary interests, is given a half-score; thus the poor receive only a half-score, since the program has benefitted only some poor, not the poor as a class, and because the level of benefits has been low. The OIP is not scored at all because its low level of results do not permit scoring. By contrast the middle class and organized labor have received low-level direct and indirect benefits. Business has generally received direct and high-level benefits from the RRC, BAC, and PPC programs.

Several important conclusions can be drawn from the data in Table 7-5. First, a diversity of political power holders seems to be indicated by column one; business is not the greatest initiator of programs, and a variety of governmental bodies, both state and local, are included in the government column. Yet this column shows simply who planned programs and called meetings; while this is important it is no more important than the question of who controlled the agency, who gave it its priorities, or whose priorities the agency adopted, and who realized major direct benefits from the program. And it should be added that, whenever the city's mayor or manager is the initiator, as they were in the case of OIP and OEDC, then given the degree of influence of the *Tribune* over city elections, the city's leading business elite can be called the indirect decision-makers (see Chapter One).

A final important empirical discovery is shown by column two, where business shows itself to have a greater frequency of executive control over programs than does government itself. Table 7-5 shows that business holds exclusive administrative control in the case of BAC; and that businessmen held important or final decision authority, through an executive committee in the case of PPC and OIP, or as top leader of a governmental agency in the case of RRC and the first phase of the poverty program (OEDC). In the latter phase of the war on poverty there has been a three-way division of authority.

Indeed in columns two and three business or corporate activists score for every agency and program and are the only groups to have this 100 percent scoring record. Quite manifestly, the finding of Robert Dahl in New Haven, R. Schultz in "Cibola," and M. Kent Jennings in Atlanta that economic dominants (big business) had withdrawn from city politics is not borne out in Oakland; while the arguments of the power structuralists find direct confirmation. This power of business generally and of activist corporations in particular, with their ability to promote industrial as opposed to social priorities, suggests that the term "governing class" is an appropriate term for describing business influence over poverty-related programs in the city since 1945.

NOTES

1 A brief outline of the functions of the State Planning Board is given in a Radio Address of Dr. Samuel C. May, Chairman, California State Planning Board, Thursday, April 3, 1941. Institute of Governmental Studies Library collection, Berkeley.

2. For analyses of what happened to NRPB, see: Charles E. Merriam, "The National Resources Planning Board: A Chapter in American Planning Experience,' *American Political Science Review,* December 1944, pp. 1075-1089,

Rexford G. Tugwell, *The Democratic Roosevelt,* Garden City, N.Y.: Doubleday, 1957, p. 612; and David Cushman Coyle, "The American National
Planning Board," (London) *Political Quarterly,* May 1945, pp. 246-252, esp.
247.

3. Mel Scott, *The San Francisco Bay Area: A Metropolis in Perspective,*
   Berkeley: University of California, 1959, p. 261-262.

4. At the same time the commission submitted over 50 studies on a variety of
   postwar reconversion planning problems, including two major reports on
   conversion to peacetime employment, and adopted liberal recommendations
   for such measures as an increase of Federal minimum wage to 65 cents an
   hour and the creation of on-the-job training programs. Source: Reconstruction and Reemployment Commission, *Report and Recommendations for year
   ending December 3, 1945,* pp. 119-126.

5. Mel Scott, op. cit.

6. A. J. Mount, an important figure in city bond campaigns during the thirties.
   and John F. Hassler, Oakland's City Manager from 1932 to 1941 and from
   1946 to 1954, were also officers in the Central Bank. For officials of the first
   Bay Region Council see Scott, op. cit., p. 262.

7. A full list of the main officers of the council in 1964-1965 is as follows: S. C.
   Beise, Chairman, Executive Committee, Bank of America; Cyril Magnin,
   President, Joseph Magnin Co.; William E. Roberts, President, Ampex Cor-
   poration; Howard G. Vesper, President, Standard Oil Company of California;
   Wendel Witter, Partner, Dean Witter and Company; Ralph Larson, President
   Morris Plan of California; Albert E. Schwabacher, Jr., Senior Partner, Schwa-
   bacher and Company; E. L. DeMattei, Assistant Treasurer; Southern Pacific
   Company; and John C. Lilly and Stanley McCaffrey, listed as "Bay Area
   Council." The Council had, in addition to its main officers three governing
   bodies including: County Vice-Presidents (nine members, seven banking and
   business, two publishers) and the Board of Governors (see Table 7-1, above).
   The Board of Governors is the most "representative" in that it includes the
   largest cross section of the business community and the greatest number of
   nonbusiness members, of all of the council's governing bodies. Source: Bay
   Area Council, *Bay Area Council, 1964-1965 Officers,* San Francisco, 1964.

8. ABAG is comprehensive in scope, like the council. Single-purpose planning
   groups created between 1945 and 1965 include the Water Pollution Control
   Board (1949), Bay Area Rapid Transit District (1957) and the Bay Development and Conservation Commission (1965). The pollution districts have not
   taken any strong enforcement measures against private or public corporations.

9. Postwar Planning Committee, *Oakland's Formula for the Future,* 1945, pp.
   11-12.

10. Oakland *Tribune,* May 7, 1945.

11. Postwar Planning Committee, op. cit., p. 55.

12. J. M. Regal, *Oakland's Partnership for Change,* Oakland: Department of
    Human Resources, 1967. This monograph is the official evaluation of the

Ford Foundation's activity in Oakland, written by the research director of the city's poverty program.

13. Wayne Thompson, "Developing a City's Human Resources," *Public Management*, 45, No. 4, April 1963, pp. 76 and 78.

14. For other analysis of Oakland's poverty program see Judy May, doctoral dissertation in progress, University of California, Berkeley, Department of Political Science; and Ralph Kramer, *Participation of the Poor, Comparative Community Case Studies in the War on Poverty*, Englewood Cliffs, N. J.: Prentice-Hall, 1969.

15. Oakland Economic Development Council, *Minutes*, December 23, 1964, pp. 1-2.

16. U.S. Senate Committee on Labor and Welfare, *Examination of the War on Poverty, Staff and Consultants Report, Vol. VII* (Oakland), prepared for the Subcommittee on Employment, Manpower, and Poverty, 90th Cong. Washington: GPO, September 1967, p. 2203.

17. Reverend Leslie Larson, interview, January 19, 1966.

18. By contrast, San Francisco spent over $2 million in community organizing in one year, June 1965 to June 1966. Thus a city with a little over twice Oakland's population was spending almost seven times as much money on organizing.

19. East Oakland Parish, "Application for Funds under Title II-A of the Economic Opportunity Act of 1964," January 25, 1965.

20. Reverend Leslie Larson, interview cited.

21. OEDC, *Community Forum, Minutes,* November 1965, p. 3.

22. Reverend Brad Bryant, Chairman, Fruitvale TAAC, interview, January 25, 1966.

23. (Oakland Economic Development Commission) *Reporter,* October-November 1967, p. 1.

24. Yet the city maintains a strong political influence. As of late 1970 the mayor had control over 13 members of the 39-member OEDC. Source: OEDCI, "Discover Oakland, The Friendly City," as quoted in Oakland *Tribune,* August 11, 1970.

25. Shortly after the Nixon administration took office in 1968 the regional OEO began to raise objections to funding the Oakland OEDCI; Moore successfully answered all criticisms leveled against his administration by the regional office. See Oakland *Tribune,* December 31, 1969.

26. At a press conference called in December of 1969 in response to the police killings of Black Panthers in Chicago, one caucus member defended the Panthers as the vanguard of the black community; another pointed to the police as puppets of the business community. See *People's World,* January 3, 1970, p. 8.

27. Daniel Moynihan, *Maximum Feasible Misunderstanding, Community Action in the War on Poverty,* New York: Free Press, 1970, pp. 136-137 and passim.

28. Two volumes contain the essential liberal critique: Daniel Moynihan, ed., *On Understanding Poverty,* New York: Basic Books, 1969, is written largely by

the academics whose writings influenced the poverty program directly or indirectly: Herbert Gans, Oscar Lewis, Lee Rainwater, Harold Watts, Stephen Thernstrom. James L. Sundquist, ed., *On Fighting Poverty,* New York: Basic Books, 1969, is written by those who designed and administered the OEO, including Robert Coles, Sanford Kravitz, and Adam Yarmolinsky. Structural analyses of poverty which imply the inability of OEO to deal with root causes of poverty are in Barry Bluestone, "The Poor Who *Have* Jobs," *Dissent,* 15, no. 5, September-October 1968, pp. 410-419; Hymen Lumer, *Poverty, Its Roots and Its Future,* New York: International Publishers, 1965; and J. Larner and I. Howe, *Poverty, Views from the Left,* New York: Morrow, 1968.

CHAPTER EIGHT

The Politics of Poverty, III:

Control and Content of Job Creation and Training Programs, 1958–1971

Less than one year after the Castlemont and Technical High School outbreaks, a small group of local businessmen began work on the first postwar employment program initiated at the local level. Eight years later, Oakland's new Mayor, John Reading, was publicly announcing that jobs and employment were the *most* important problems in the city and had created a manpower commission to consider them, sponsored a Job Fair in cooperation with the *Tribune* and major local employers, and briefly—before reversing himself—supported the demand of a local black group, JOBART, for increasing the number of black workers employed in the construction of the Bay Area Rapid Transit system.[1] Thus the city recognized for the first time that jobs and employment should have top priority on the city agenda. The questions were now, belatedly, moved to a new level: how serious was the city's commitment to attacking the employment problem? And, given the relative unconcern of the majority of the city's large private employers, would the political-economic system be willing to move toward a real solution?

MANPOWER PROGRAMS AND FEDERAL AID TO OAKLAND

Over 140 Federal programs were spending money in Oakland during 1967, at an annual rate of almost $100 million.[2] About two dozen programs and about $24 million in Federal spending in the county were channeled specifically into poverty and job training programs in 1966. There were some 13 federally funded manpower-related programs supported entirely by five Federal agencies. The particular recipients of this Federal largesse are shown in Table 8-1.[3]

Small business was also included, on a miniscule scale, in the Federal grant program. The distribution of funds shown in Table 8-1 allows several observations. First, by placing so much money directly with the

TABLE 8-1   *Direct recipients of Federal and state grants for job creating programs in Oakland, as of April 1, 1967*

Big business (four corporations)	$ 6,880,000
Government (five local and county agencies)	10,950,000
Organized labor (Alameda County Central Labor Council)	1,500,000
Minorities groups (three groups)	158,000
Negro ministers (one group)	60,000
Small business (two groups)	185,000
Mixed (business, labor, minorities)	4,600,000
Total	$24,333,000

Source for Tables 8-1 and 8-2: Fact sheet prepared by Hugh Taylor, Special Assistant for Manpower, "Major Manpower Programs Operating in Oakland," March 29, 1967.

Note: Figures include total aid promised by Economic Development Administration as of April 1968.

giant corporations, the programs were based on the premise that subsidizing big business for training programs was a better approach to the
job problem than subsidizing small business or creating new industry.
Yet in fact, job training programs only opens up existing jobs for
hard-core workers; it does nothing to increase the total job supply.
Secondly, by directing the grants to the corporations and government
bodies the Federal government avoided any buildup of a small business
or poor people's political base of opposition to existing elected officials. A well-organized Corporation of the Poor was in existence in the
city during the mid and late 1960s, created with the help of white-
collar professionals, and ready to establish small-scale privately and
cooperatively run businesses. Yet all of the proposals of the Corporation of the Poor for Federal money were turned down, and no job
program went to them. Had small businessmen, or the Corporation,
realized even a fraction of the $600,000 of profits guaranteed to
Lytton Industries for running the Job Corps, there would have been

TABLE 8-2 *Income range of proprietors
of first 64 recipients of
SBDC loans, March 1-
December 31, 1966*

Income ($)	Number	Percent
under 3,000	22	34.3
3,000-4,000	22	34.3
5,000-7,499	17	26.7
7,500-9,999	3	4.7
10,000 or more	0	0.0

Source: Oakland Small Business Development Center,
Inc., "Selected Sociological Characteristics of Successful Borrowers: March 1-December 31, 1966."

enough money to finance a number of significant political campaigns at the city and county level. Hence by its choice of recipient administrators the Federal government reinforced the existing structure of power of the county.

Its choice of recipients also reinforced the influence of the liberal-to-moderate political ideology of these recipient institutions. The minority groups referred to in Table 8-1 include the Urban League and the Indian Association, neither of which qualify as militant. The revolutionary wing of the county labor movement was purged in the 1950s, so that the approaches of labor, minority, and business groups to the city's problems all fell within an establishment consensus. Policy rivalry within this framework arose over such questions as which group would control the Skill Center, and the wage levels and working conditions of blue collar employees at the Job Corps facility. In each case disputes were nonideological and of limited scope.

The Power and Control of Advisory Committees

The basic power to set policy for all Federal grants lies in Washington. Yet the local level is involved in the detailed structuring of program. The political interests and lines of influence of the local mayors and elected officials have been traced in Chapter One. Here we examine the memberships of the important policy and advisory committees of seven agencies having a manpower or job training or job creation mission: The OEDC; Manpower Development and Training Act Council; Skill Center Advisory Council; the Oakland Adult Minority Employment Advisory Council; On-the-job Training Advisory Council; the mayor of Oakland's Manpower Commission; and the Small Business Development Center (SBDC). Figures for all of these councils are based on their composition as of 1967.[4] In each case the word "advisory" is somewhat misleading, since each had direct and primary policy making authority over its program.

As Table 8-3 shows, large and medium-sized businesses each account for 53 of all advisory committee positions, heavily outweighing the number of working poor. It is also noteworthy that the majority of advisory committee members came from the same congeries of trade unions, downtown-based civil rights groups, and giant corporations already active in the city's politics. The fact that the Urban League, Mexican American Political Association, and the NAACP, groups which are conservative in tactics and ideology, claimed almost all of the appointments in the civil rights category suggests a permanent pattern of power and manipulation from the top of the political system. Other nonwhite political groups exist, notably the militant Oakland Black Caucus, but never received any appointments. Kaiser Industries, through the work of three very active employees, claimed a total of seven positions on job advisory committees. No other company claimed as many.

The pattern of appointments is crucial in two respects. First, by limiting his appointment to reliable nonwhite organizations, the mayor, who had greater responsibility for appointments to such committees than any other person, could play politics in his selection process. Only

TABLE 8-4   Economic and professional backgrounds of job advisory committee members, 1966-1968

Source: Complied from membership lists supplied by the advisory committees.

*Also includes very small businesses. Crosshatched area refers to OEDC poor members.

†Includes well-established local firms and professionals (doctors, lawyers, etc.).

**Refers only to representatives of the following corporations: Pacific Gas and Electric Company, Pacific Telephone, Kaiser Industries, World Airways, San Francisco Bay Area Council, and Gerber Products.

one black appointee of the mayor ever crossed him publicly in the years 1965-1970; indeed for young blacks in the city the Urban League and the NAACP have the appearance of being part of the ruling system. Moreover, out of 115 job-related advisory positions, only 25 were held by individuals who were not attached to a political or civic parent organization, such as a downtown business club or the League of Women Voters; perhaps 40 percent of all advisory committee members were members of the Oakland Chamber of Commerce, the largest single organizational affiliation, followed by labor with about 25 percent and the NAACP with over 15 percent. Thus business had the largest bloc of appointments on advisory committees, while appointments came always from a definite set of politically active organizations in town. This is a kind of pluralism of organizational affiliations, but with business as the most active class. And the mayor, himself a small industrialist, was at the top of the heirarchy, in command of much of the selection process. The correct description for this is political elitism. Today there is pressure on the mayor to appoint minorities from *all* political groups and ideologies, a policy which would amount to a more genuine pluralism in appointments policy.

THE MINORITY EMPLOYMENT PROJECT: LOCAL FAILURE

Prior to 1958, job-related programs had been special programs run by state agencies. The U.S. Bureau of Indian Affairs, located in Oakland, trains some American Indians for nonunion jobs. Unemployment among Indians remains high. The State of California trains and finds jobs for the vocationally handicapped, and through its department of employment acts as a job clearinghouse. The first corporate effort in the city to provide jobs, titled Operation Bootstrap and undertaken in the mid-1950s, offered little more than simple encouragement to the poor to better themselves.

In 1958 the city's corporate elite developed its most ambitious program of the postwar period. In that year the Oakland Adult Minority Employment Project, the first program to deal seriously with the problems of unemployment in general and Negro unemployment in particular, began life with the meetings of a group of businessmen which began roughly two years before the official Project started. This group apparently was quite concerned with the comparatively high tax rate in Oakland which they felt was related to the large number of people, most of whom were Negroes, receiving welfare payments.[5]

The main initiators of this private group seem to have been a Kaiser executive and a local realtor. It was this unofficial group which tried to create its own, private employment agency for unemployed blacks and which ended up by placing the program under the administrative control of the state Department of Employment.[6]

The initial business nucleus was expanded to include labor and conservative civil rights groups including the NAACP and the Urban League. The then President of the NAACP became chairman of this advisory committee which also included some of the most important business leaders in town. Three special offices for employing Negroes were set up, *outside* the state Department of Employment main office, staffed by people specially screened for high motivation for finding jobs for minorities. Job developers were hired to track down available employers in the Oakland area willing to offer jobs to people with police records and other employment liabilities. Business representation was substantial on the advisory committee, based on business' own argument that it, business, had the necessary liaison with local employers to open up jobs. The committee sent out hundreds of letters to employers explaining the program and asking for support. Originated by business, enjoying financial support from the state and from the U.S. Department of Labor, in addition to editorial support from the Oakland Tribune, the project represented the first concerted postwar effort to deal with unemployment. Its performance is highly significant.

In operation both the advisory committee and the three special project offices began to develop problems quite early in their careers. The advisory committee was wracked by factionalism between the labor and business representatives, which limited the effectiveness of the committee's operation and, according to one close observer, allowed the California State Employment Service (CSES) to set its own course.[7] The job developers were unable to develop, or locate, the number of jobs which the business community originally had estimated as available in the community. As a result no greater a percentage of hard-core* Negro unemployed found employment through the project than through the main office of the state Department of Employment. Above all, the success of the project depended on the willingness of local employers to go to the project for employees, to employ men whose skill or police records made them somewhat greater risks as employees. According to the official interim evaluation of the project, the business community was not prepared to take that risk and continued to place most of its orders for employees at the main office.

As a result of these frustrations the job developers gradually shifted their goals from finding jobs for the hard-core unemployed, to the easier task of finding jobs for the qualified unemployed. This, of course, was the same order of priorities which local employers, with cooperation of the CSES, had always been following, and which had contributed to the problem of hard-core unemployment in the first place. Lacking any funds for job creation, the project in its first six months had succeeded in finding jobs for only 91 men and 32 women out of over 2,500 unemployed persons who came to it looking for work.[8] Most of these jobs were in the low-skilled categories. Moreover, they were found with employers already represented on the project's advisory committee, who presumably needed no further persuasion as to the reality of the employment problem. The policies of the bulk of the city's employers remained, under this voluntary program, quite unchanged. The entire program could have accomplished practically everything that it did achieve had it stopped with the selection of an advisory committee and never undertaken the extensive, and expensive, job development effort.

THE FAILURE OF FEDERAL PROGRAMS

The Skill Center

As originally announced by the state Department of Employment in 1966, the Skill Center was to provide training for 1,500 unemployed, at

---

*Hard-core unemployment may be taken to refer to any person unemployed for over 12 months and who has a police record or record of bad employment or a lack of basic education. The advisory committee struggled over the question of a definition of hard-core and arrived at no specific definition. The above definition includes the major elements discussed by the committee.

an initial cost of $5 million paid jointly by Manpower Development and Training Act* and Economic Development Act funds. It was announced by the state Department of Employment at a meeting of the advisory council of the Manpower Development and Training Act, a council where business and labor representatives shared membership almost equally. The Skill Center idea was broached during a council meeting which almost no labor representatives were attending, due to a conflicting special meeting of county labor leaders. Partly because the state announced this large program at a meeting from which they were perforce absent, and partly from fear that training the unemployed would lead to competition for *existing* jobs and thereby threaten the whole basis of apprenticeship programs by which labor theretofore had kept a monopoly on the job supply, the county's labor leaders brought a strong protest to the state's Democratic governor, Edmond "Pat" Brown. As a result of this protest the number of job categories for which training was to be supplied was reduced to seven, and the county labor council was put in charge of selecting a director for the center, a procedure which guaranteed that there would be no conflict between center programs and the wishes of organized labor.

In practice, the Skill Center was as great a fiasco as the Adult Minority Employment Project. As announced by the district's Congressman in 1966, the center was to have $3.9 million for 800 enrollees, a little over half the original projection. Before the program had been operating six months another cutback in these funds was announced, shortening the basic education program for trainees—many of whom were functionally illiterate—from 20 to less than 6 weeks and cutting each enrollee's allowance from $6,000 to $4,000. By necessity this meant the hard-core unemployed would no longer be a part of the program. The smaller allowance could not sustain trainees for much over 24 months. As the chairman of the MDTA advisory council put it, "A thirty-six week training program is insufficient to help the hard-core. We do not need short-term training programs in the East Bay any longer."[9] A memo by three center staff members put the question

---

*The Manpower Development and Training Act, passed by Congress in 1962, and operated by the U.S. Department of Labor, provided Federal funds for retraining of the unemployed to fill existing job vacancies. All funds spent in any district are first approved by a local MDTA advisory council, on which labor has a substantial representation. For a list of MDTA programs in Alameda County see p. 174.

more tartly: "Is the federal government just interested in retraining the 'cream of the unemployed,' or are they going to attack the real unemployment problem—retraining the hard-core unemployed?"[10] In 1970, the Skill Center was still in operation, training several hundred unemployed in a city where some 15,000 men and women were now unemployed.[11] The length of the training program remained basically unchanged.

Other MDTA Programs

Another whole set of retraining programs, under MDTA, has been carried on in Alameda County, as indicated in Table 8-4.

In none of the job training programs listed in Table 8-4 would the trainees enjoy union status on completion of their program. As a Naval Air Station spokesman put it, the trainee "will become a journeyman

TABLE 8-4   MDTA project sponsors and job descriptions for major training projects, August 1966 to March 1967

		FEPC record	
Sponsors	Job descriptions	Complaints	Convictions
A naval air station	200 aircraft maintenance workers	1	0
A county nurses association	Upgrade skills of Registered Nurses	0	0
A major airline	510 aircraft maintenance men	1	1
A Federal economic development agency	Clerical training	—	—
A private gas and electric company	Train utility workers	32	9
A state employment agency	Train 15 window displaymen	40	13
Oakland Adult Minority Employment Project	Train 150 auto repairmen and service station attendants	—	—

Source: Alameda County MDTA Advisory Council, *Minutes* for August 25, 1966, November 30, 1966, and March 8, 1967. Source of FEPC record: FEPC files, San Francisco.

when an opening occurs for which he is qualified and *if promoted*" (emphasis added). And, as the table indicates, several of the agencies receiving Federal job training funds had been found by the state Fair Employment Practices Committee (FEPC) to be guilty of racial discrimination in their own employment policies, findings which never interrupted the flow of MDTA funds. Thus MDTA could claim the dubious distinction of publicly subsidizing racially discriminatory employers.

Economic Development Administration: "To Create a Climate Conducive to the Development of Private Enterprise"[12]

In 1965 the Economic Development Administration (EDA), successor to the old Area Redevelopment Administration in the Department of Commerce, began shaping a program for Oakland. In this new approach, development money was to be given directly to private business in the forms of loans and grants, on condition that recipient corporations take a certain percentage of their new hirees from the hard-core unemployed. The authorizing legislation made it clear that the long-term unemployed, and not just the jobless, would be a principal object of concern, a position reiterated by the Oakland office. And unlike any earlier program, the EDA intended not simply to retrain the unemployed but to provide a substantial number of new, permanent jobs.[13]

At the national level, the founding of the program did not provide much grounds for encouragement. Partly due to the opposition of the U.S. Chamber of Commerce to the whole EDA concept, the national program received a shoestring $800,000 appropriation for its first year of existence. And it was placed in the Department of Commerce, traditionally dominated by large corporations, despite the vigorously expressed preference of the bill's sponsor, Senator Paul Douglas of Illinois, to give the program to an independent agency.[14]

In Oakland the new program initially gave promise of putting some Federal money into the poor neighborhoods. On his first visit to Oakland the local EDA administrator, Eugene Foley, went first to the flatlands leaders and then to city hall, an order of visits which irritated local officials. Amory Bradford was Foley's chief assistant in Oakland. Bradford was a former executive of the New York *Times* and an economic liberal. An insight into the purposes, and weaknesses, of the program occurred during an exchange between Bradford and a member of the audience at a meeting of the West Oakland TAAC:

Bradford: The idea of this (Economic Development) Act is to provide permanent jobs—not just the kind that come with building a court-house ... It takes about $10,000 of financing to create each new job.

Question from audience: But Moore Paints is moving out of town this year and is taking several hundred jobs with it. What will EDA do about that?

Bradford: Some movement in local plants is inevitable. We can't restrict business from moving; all EDA can do is to induce business to stay in town by offering financial inducements.[15]

Yet in the actual shaping of the program the flatlands groups were not consulted. During the first weeks in which the basic decisions were made Bradford met primarily with officials of the city manager's office, the Oakland Port Authority, and members of the chamber of commerce. He went back to the black community only *after* the allocation of funds was decided. The flatlands groups did not get a penny and

TABLE 8-5   *EDA-approved grants and loans for Oakland, as of December 31, 1967 (amounts in thousands of dollars)*

Recipient	Grants	Loans	Technical assistance grants
Port of Oakland	7,789	5,144	40
World Airways	6,390	4,260	
City of Oakland	414	–	61
Bank of America, Charter Bank of London (combined)	–	225	–
Small, medium business	1,124	–	146
Other	–	–	466
Totals	15,717	9,629	713
GRAND TOTAL, ALL GRANTS AND LOANS			26,059

Source: Compiled from Economic Development Administration, *Directory of Approved Projects as of December 31, 1967*, Washington: U.S. Department of Commerce, December 31, 1967, pp. 8-9.

blasted Bradford, to his face, as a hypocrite. The program as announced in 1968 is shown in Table 8-5.

Both Foley and Bradford cautioned the city against expecting rapid results from EDA investments.[16] Creating permanent jobs could not be done overnight. They set the requirement that businesses benefiting from EDA grants or loans should take a certain percentage of new hires from the hard-core unemployed, and to oversee this provision EDA created a review panel of business and civil rights representatives. The panel had no enforcement powers, however, and has played an almost insignificant role in the program.

For medium and large business, EDA was an immediate boon. The stock of World Airways, a major recipient of EDA money, went from $32 to almost $64 a share the day after EDA announced its Oakland program. Yet, overall, the program, like other programs in the city, has shown a limited result. It never *required* that its business recipients go to the Adult Minority Employment Project to get employees, a failure which made it easier for businesses to evade their promises to employ the hard core. The review panel never was given any power to enforce compliance, and EDA never followed up its initial interest in funding the Skills Center. By early 1970 the program had earmarked $32 million for the city, and had spent only $7 million, including $2.1 for an industrial park on port land and another $1.5 million for the West Oakland Health Center. And the program has not come close to creating the 2,000 permanent jobs it initially promised. Any exact evaluation of job creation is made difficult by the fact that EDA does not issue any figures on the number of permanent jobs it claims to have created.

CONCLUSION

Two kinds of conclusions can be drawn from the city's 12-year experience with employment programs. The first relates to the content of the programs, the other, to their control.

1. The Federal government, despite the 1946 Employment Act, has not committed itself to the goal of full employment. Hence all of the federally funded programs in the city have been stopgap in philosophy, lacking any definite goals or guidelines for evaluation of performance.

2. Job programs have not been geared to the future shape of the East Bay economy. The failure of programs to retain any but the most employable of the unemployed is a constant theme of the past dozen years. Not only has this left thousands of the hard core without hope, it has also failed to anticipate and prepare the hard core for a share of the job market as that market will be in the year 1980—fewer unskilled jobs, more service industry jobs. It is not fair simply to criticize unions for their policy of keeping apprenticeships programs lily white. The unions, too, want to hold onto their jobs; the basic fault lies with the political and economic systems which have not provided adequate work for millions who are willing and able to work.

3. Training programs, which do not increase the job supply, have been pacifiers whose main effect is to reduce momentary political tension and create the appearance of doing something. There are far more significant programs which the Federal government, if it so desired, could undertake today. In 1966 Lyndon Johnson's Automation Commission pointed out there were over 5 million jobs waiting to be filled in the public service sector. In 1968 the Kerner Commission report recommended that 1 million of them be funded at once.[17] Instead, all Federal job money on a national basis as well as in Oakland has gone to skill centers and to private employers to train workers which they can then employ. None of the programs subsidize nongovernmental or noncorporate employment opportunities, and in fact over half of Federal job program money spent in the county has gone first to private business that is guaranteed some profit.

By contrast there are no published figures by independent agencies to show that *any* hard-core unemployed have benefited from public or private job programs, or how long retrained workers from the Skill Center stay in their new jobs, or if the training really gets them anything more than a poverty or deprivation level employment. Thus corporate industry and government have benefited considerably from the thrust of job programs in the county, while the benefits to unemployed, both the hard core and the cream, range from nothing to very little.

4. Of all the nongovernmental interest groups involved in the employment programs, large corporations played the most impor-

tant role, while the goals of employment programs sooner or later harmonized exactly with the priorities of these same corporations. Business held a substantial number of seats on all job-related advisory committees, a number far disproportionate to its numbers in the population at large. It was the direct recipient and, after government, the most frequent administrator of government employment funds, in some cases without any public advisory committee. The city's largest corporation, Kaiser, and other city businesses were the initiators of the Adult Minority Employment Project, were the close consultants of the state employment agencies in planning the Skill Center, and were the major influence on the shaping of EDA's local program, while one of the state's largest corporations was administrator of the entire Job Corps program. Business has played a secondary role as planner and administrator in three programs: WIN, Concentrated Employment Program (including New Careers), and the Skill Center. Yet, because it takes a good percentage of CEP and Skill Center trainees as employees, by refusing cooperation with these programs business could shut them down. Thus, far from withdrawing from local politics in the area of job programs, business is clearly involved as a predominant influence.

A California Senator and Oakland realtor stood in the Oakland City Council chamber 25 years ago and declared that "Industry can do the job—but government must step into the gaps." (See p. 142). Today, after several decades of experience in economic development and job programs, it is perfectly clear that industry *cannot* do the job of solving unemployment, and that together with government it has not even proposed measures which could insure a job for the 15,000 unemployed in Oakland.

NOTES

1. This defense of JOBART (Justice on Bay Area Rapid Transit) is the only time, to this writer's knowledge, that any mayor in Oakland directly defended the specific demands of a black group. JOBART demanded that the additional workers needed to build the multimillion dollar rapid transit system be trained from among the city's unemployed, and not be imported from out-of-state unions. Neither the directors of BART, nor the local building trades unions appreciated the mayor's position and within six

months the mayor had modified his stance considerably. The mayor's letter to BART defending the JOBART proposals is in *Flatlands,* June 18-July 1, 1966, p. 8. See also Patrick J. Mahoney, "Minority Employment in the Construction of BART," San Francisco, CORO Foundation, July 1966.

2. Statement by Mayor John H. Reading, Mayor of Oakland; in hearings by Senate Committee on Government Operations, Subcommittee on Executive Reorganization, *Federal Role in Urban Affairs,* 1967, part 4, pp. 818-819.

3. In addition to the programs shown in Table 8-1, which were specifically designed for Oakland, the county was headquarters for two Federal programs designed to serve several Western states. The Job Corps was administered by Lytton Industries at Camp Parks, under a contract from OEO which guaranteed the corporation a 6 percent rate of profit, or almost $1 million. The Nixon administration phased this project out in 1969. The Western headquarters of the Bureau of Indian Affairs is in Oakland, with a $2 million program for training Indians for largely menial, nonunionized jobs.

4. The city has had other important job programs operating since 1967. The Concentrated Employment Program (CEP), operating under the OEDC, was funded in 1969 for about $3.5 million, of which about $500,000 went to New Careers, an on-the-job training program with both public and private employers which seems to have worked well. It has placed some 3,000 workers. The Work Incentive Program (WIN) in 1969 cost $400,000 and had 350 participants; the mayor's office claims to have provided, in the same year, 12,000 summer jobs for youth, and the National Alliance of Businessmen claims that, nation-wide, it has filled positions for 6,300 persons, although it is not clear that these are positions that would not have been filled without NAB. Source: City of Oakland, *Oakland Urban Renewal, Workable Program,* Oakland, 1969, pp. 8-d and 8-e.

5. Dr. William B. Woodson, co-author (with Susan S. Sheffield) of the interim evaluations of the Adult Minority Employment Project, interview, May 1967.

6. An alternative arrangement, putting the project in the hands of a private employment agency, was defeated by the then-president of the NAACP, who was included in the early stages of planning of the Project. William Woodson, interview, May 1967.

7. Dr. William B. Woodson, interview, January 21, 1966.

8. William B. Woodson and Susan S. Sheffield, *Interim Report of the Oakland Adult Project Follow-Up Study,* Oakland, Department of Human Resources, June 1966, p. 19.

9. Alameda County MDTA Advisory Council, *Minutes,* November 30, 1966.

10. Oakland *Flatlands,* June 18, 1966, p. 5.

11. Mayor Reading testified to this figure at hearings before the Senate subcommittee on manpower programs. Oakland *Tribune,* April 19, 1970.

12. This quotation represents a major purpose of the EDA program as outlined in U.S. House of Representatives, Committee on Public Works, "Highlights of the Public Works and Economic Development Act of 1965," Washington: GPO, 1965, p. 3.

13. The legislation creating EDA states that EDA-aided private investment will "(1) tend to improve opportunities for the successful establishment or expansion of industrial or commercial facilities; (2) otherwise assist in the creation of additional long-term employment opportunities in the area; or (3) primarily benefit the long-term unemployed and members of low-income families or otherwise substantially further the objectives of the Economic Opportunities Act." Public Law 89-136, 89th Cong., S. 1648, Title I, Sec. 101(a), August 26, 1965.

14. The head of the Department of Commerce at the time the EDA was established was John Conner. Conner, just prior to heading Commerce, was president (at $129,000 a year salary) of the giant pharmaceutical company, Merck and Company and vice-chairman of the Business (Advisory) Council. For a biography see *Fortune* magazine, February 1965, p. 47. The opposition of the U.S. Chamber of Commerce to the Douglas bill is noted in Sar Levitan, *Federal Aid to Depressed Areas,* Baltimore: Johns Hopkins, 1964, p. 9.

15. Meeting of the West Oakland TAAC, February 8, 1966, attended by the author.

16. For this detail, and other facts relating to the process of creation of the EDA, the author is indebted to Dr. Floyd Hunter, a consultant to EDA throughout its early years. For an alternative account of the EDA program see Amory Bradford, *Oakland's Not for Burning,* New York: McKay, 1968.

17. *Report of the National Advisory Commission on Civil Disorders* (Kerner Commission), New York: Bantam Books, 1968, p. 417.

3

The Uses of Urban Power

CONCLUSION

Who Rules, and for Whom?

No political system is static, certainly not that of Oakland. The first part of this concluding section will review briefly the evolution of urban politics as a way of understanding the present nature of Oakland's power system.

By the turn of the century, the evolution of the economic system in the northern states had brought a nouveau riche of industrial, commercial, and real estate interests onto the urban political scene. The representatives of these interests in eastern cities were well able to influence the ethnic politicians who had largely displaced from politics the earlier commercial-social elite. The increasing political power of these new interests developed across the continent as industrial development spread to the Pacific shore.

In contrast to this view of economic influence, political science has viewed the rise of the new ethnic politicians as signaling the *end* of elitism in American urban politics. These writers have quite accurately stressed the fact of displacement, of the demise of the old social aristocracy from its direct control of political office. And historians have added to this displacement thesis by showing that, by the year 1912, the (Marxist) Socialist party held about 1,200 local offices, including 79 mayors, in over 300 American cities and towns.[1] None of the Socialist Party officeholders were from the old social elite, and many were from the working class. Here, clearly, displacement was the major fact.

Yet what is overlooked in these interpretations of displacement is how largely local governments, run by ethnic politicians, functioned as instruments serving the interests of the growing urban industrial and real estate groups. Corruption of urban politicians by business interests, one of the factors which caused such outrage in Oakland and turned public sentiment in favor of a city manager system, has been amply documented by numerous historians and muckrakers as a basic part of ethnic politics. Similarly, the fact that present-day corporations do not frequently run candidates for office and directly staff elective positions in city government does not prevent the urban political system from serving the basic interests of the urban corporation, nor does it prevent corporate managers from playing a decisive role in city politics when they so choose. Business involvement in urban redevelopment has been documented in many cities; in Pittsburgh, the regional businessmen's association was the spearhead for completely redeveloping, and largely eliminating pollution from, the Golden Triangle of downtown Pittsburgh. Freeway, airport, and sports development have been pushed by urban businessmen across the country. It was the Chairman of the Board of U.S. Steel, Roger Blough, whose corporation normally remains out of sight on civil rights activity, who was widely credited with putting pressure on the city of Birmingham—where U.S. Steel is headquartered—to allow Martin Luther King to lead a protest march during the tense days in 1965. Rarely in the literature of community power do any researchers find that organized labor assumes the leading role in politics; most urban officeholders are of the small business and middle classes. Hence, to reformulate, even though the chairman of U.S. Steel is not himself mayor or city councilman, the mayors and councilmen can still represent U.S. Steel's basic interests in politics, and be open to specific initiative from the corporation on any political subject, including the right of blacks to hold a protest march.

In Oakland, the development of urban capitalism played a crucial role as it had in the industrial northeastern states, but under somewhat different circumstances. Like many other western cities, Oakland had small-propertied mayors from the beginning of its history. Before the turn of the century the city lacked the economic affluence necessary to develop a social or economic aristocracy remotely comparable to the Cabots or Bidwells. The development of such a social class took place for the first time with the growth of industrialism in the decades preceding and following the First World War, and was confirmed by the founding of the exclusive Athens Athletic Club in the 1920s, decades after the formation of its Eastern analogues such as the Links Club in New York. Furthermore, Oakland's political system has been affected by the fact that the city never was faced with the sudden influx of nonassimilated European or Asian ethnics. The vast majority of its growing industrial class were second or third or fourth generation Americans, many of them already of the intellectual or small-business classes, who came West to make their fortunes. These early settlers, men-on-the-make like Horace Carpentier, found no established social-political structure to displace and so created their own. Hence the ethnic factor did not play as great a role as in Eastern cities.

The city did develop a power structure in which, historically, small businessmen have made many decisions. The present mayor is owner of a medium- sized food products factory; of the businessmen represented in Table 2-7, the majority are small businessmen engaged in retail or real estate operations. One member of the redevelopment commission is owner of a small stationery store, a member of the city council has a small appliance store, and others are lawyers and realtors. Yet, while these men are of the middle-class or small-business groups, they are not spokesmen in any sense for the interests of small business as a whole on major questions such as taxation. They receive appointments and, with *Tribune* endorsement, they win elections. But the electoral influence of the paper prevents them from taking any great independent role. A major assault on slum property decay and urban rejuvenation would probably find them, along with their associates in the real estate industry, in opposition.

The most crucial potential for the city's politics is with organized and unorganized labor, whose white racial composition during the first half of this century is now being substantially altered by influxes of blacks and browns at the lowest levels of the job hierarchy. How to govern labor is a major question facing any political system, and in Oakland one can see that this question has been answered in a way that minimizes the political influence of organized labor and of the rank and file. Before the CIO period, a few labor leaders were almost always in positions of political authority, either on the city council or on boards; these leaders were always nonmilitant and their thinking on local labor questions was close to that of local employers. This formula was altered by the period of CIO organizing in the 1930s and 1940s. Today labor, which largely built and today largely runs the county Democratic party, is better able to protect itself against injunctions and the use of police by the city to break strikes, but the injunction is still easy to get and frequently used.

Labor's direct influence has been enlarged somewhat on city boards; labor leaders now can be assured of one appointment (including the chairmanship) to the port commission and to the civil service commission, the two city agencies most directly concerned with city hiring practices. In years when Democrats control the state governorship and legislature, which generally has been the case since 1956, labor leaders get prestigious and high-paying—although not always highly powerful—appointments on state boards of concern to labor. And with the election of a Democratic majority to the legislature, local labor leaders have access to the state machinery which provides occasional victories for determined labor leaders while cementing their grip over the voting of the rank and file.[2] In county board elections, the Committee on Political Education (COPE) endorses and works for Democratic candidates who occasionally win. But in city elections COPE's influence is minimal. Strictly labor candidates, talking up issues of interest to labor and clearly identified with the central labor council, have not won election to the city council since the rebellion of 1947-1951. Only small businessmen and professionals win election to the council, maintaining the pattern of the pre-CIO period.

THE SYSTEMIC INFLUENCE OF BUSINESS

Despite the economic background of the present city councilmen and board members, middle-level businessmen do not play the same predominant role in the city they did in the last century. Today a new set of big business interests, including a single newspaper, large national and regional corporations, and a developed real estate industry, has emerged as part of the city's political scene. It is the question of the relations of the economic dominants to city policy making that has drawn the greatest amount of controversy in the community power literature. What does Oakland's past and current history tell us about this relationship?

To answer this central question it is convenient to divide business influence into two areas, which may be called respectively, systemic and specialized influence. Systemic influence refers to how the business system and its activity affects the basic structure of government, or helps to draw absolute limits to policy alternatives. Specialized influence refers to influence over the selection or rejection of policies in specific areas such as economic development, welfare, planning, etc. We will first discuss systemic influence in the areas of elections, governmental structure, taxation, and general bond issues.

The city's governmental structure has been basically shaped by the city's economic leaders who, in the late 1920s and early 1930s, led the campaign for the council-manager form of government. This same reform payed off in a quick reduction in taxes and the replacement of a maverick mayor with a local banker wearing the cap of city manager. If such an occurrence had happened after an exchange of gunshots it could correctly be called a putsch; done peacefully it is called urban reform. In any event the consequences for the city's businessmen were highly satisfactory. The city's port lands were, at the same time, detached from direct city control and given over to an autonomous board largely composed of local businessmen. Businessmen supported the creation of the city's planning commission in 1911; the city's real estate board approved the creation of the city's public housing authority in the late 1930s, and the Bank of America, which bought most of the authority's early bonds, had an early appointee on the authority. Real estate, industrial, and commercial interests pushed for the creation of the independent redevelopment agency and for the Bay Area Rapid Transit district. Thus not only with the creation of a decentralized, council-manager system of the 1930s, but in all of the city's significant subsequent additions to its governmental structure, business has always either given approval to, or provided major political pressure for change. No other social sector in the city can claim such a decisive role in shaping the city's governmental institutions.

The same phenomenon can be seen in local elections. The elimination of the partisan ballot in 1911, the creation of at-large elections in 1933, and the political influence of the *Tribune* have made it nearly impossible for labor, articulate small-business candidates, or representatives of racial minorities to win office. The result is a system of mobilized bias. The basic policies of the city toward subordinate groups in the city, the moderate use of the injunction against labor, and the unlimited use of the police to control the flatlands go on unchecked, while the city manager is dependent on an almost entirely white, business-oriented city council. While the electoral system produces such a city council the city's businessmen have little to fear from politics.

Before leaving the area of electoral influence we must clarify the role of the city's newspaper, which has few equals in political influence among urban newspapers. Throughout the period of Joe Knowland the influence of the paper was augmented by the economic and political connections of its publisher, then a member of the city's banking fraternity and former U.S. Congressmen, and by a style of journalism which made it common for the paper not to print news which went contrary to the policy preferences of the publisher. Thus news of the 1928 paving company scandal grand jury had to be gleaned from the San Francisco press, as did most of the opposition comments on the 1933 charter amendments. The influence of the present publisher derives from a similar constellation of factors: a high degree of influence inside the local Republican party, based partly on past record as minority (and majority) leader of the U.S. Senate; and a substantial involvement in local economic and civic affairs, including active promotion of the county sports complex and high office in the county chamber of commerce. On top of this, the present publisher has inherited the paper's overwhelming influence in local electoral politics, now as a monopoly paper (see Chapter Two). That is a cumulation or pyramiding of political resources equaled only by the Kaiser companies in the city's business community. Very recently the paper has instituted a more bipartisan form of journalism, with relatively objective articles on the black community and poverty program. But any black potential mayor, barring a revolution, will have to deal, and perhaps make deals, with the city's establishment, including the paper, as a precondition to election. Even if a black mayor won election on the basis of a nonwhite majority of voters and without the paper's endorsement, it is doubtful that he could govern the city without at least the tacit support of the paper and the business community at large, particularly for the passage of bond issues.

Bond issues are another area of systemic influence of local businessmen. Given the city's limited tax base it cannot operate without periodic resort to important bond issues and, given the two-thirds voting requirement for passage of such issues, support by the city's business fraternity becomes a practical necessity.[3] Thus in 1945 the Postwar Planning Committee came to the rescue of the city by proposing and supporting two small bond issues (for $15 million each) which ultimately provided for less than one-tenth of the city's capital needs as estimated by department heads. In 1958 the president of a major port terminal corporation stepped into the leadership of the campaign for more funds for city schools, and then sat on the committee which decided how these funds should be spent. The Kaiser family, by its contributions of money, has assumed a leadership role over the city's cultural affairs, attracting private donations for the city's multimillion dollar art-cultural museum and for the city symphony orchestra. As a result the city has had a cultural renaissance, but only for those who can afford $10 tickets.

The available evidence thus indicates that, in both governmental and civic affairs, the city's business elite has stepped into the scene to spearhead campaigns for raising funds. Far from keeping this elite out of the political scene the city's politicians have been eager to receive such support, and for a simple reason. The large corporations, who use the city's public services, who feel free to leave town whenever investment opportunities seem brighter elsewhere, and who receive favored treatment in taxes and in some cases have been grossly underassessed, are viewed by city officials not as irresponsible elements of the community but as potential financial saviors. In short, one major and constant basis of corporate and financial influence over the city, aside from campaign contributions, persuasion of the county assessor, and the offering of lucrative private employment to public officials at retirement, is the considerable degree to which city government is dependent, financially and administratively, upon the cooperation of the local economic notables for passage of major bond issues and for assistance in carrying out major physical programs such as code enforcement, throughway construction, and redevelopment. The city manager's candid remarks at the time of the Interagency Project, that without the real support of public and economic leaders the program could not have gotten underway (see Chapter Seven), applies to every important program the city has undertaken.

The city's debt-level itself presents another area in which the city's political system, influenced by business, has drawn absolute limits on the possibilities of public policy. The city has a good bond rating in private markets, meaning that its bonds provide a good rate of interest and carry with them a strong guarantee of the solvency of the city. Such a credit rating is desired by bond purchasers in the private money markets; but it is largely the result of a low level of bonded indebtedness, well below that allowed by state law. This means that even the finances which could be raised by sale of bonds under present governmental procedures are not raised; hence the hospitals and public housing and development corporations that such money could support have not been built.

The tax system is also favorable to business, is influenced by it, and sets absolute limits to any program of economic reform. Business and elected or appointed officials realize a mutual self-interest: lower tax assessments and low or regressive official rates of taxation increase a politicians acceptability to local business and ease his problem of raising campaign resources or winning reappointment. The structure of taxation in the city and in the state, as described in Chapter Four, is regressive, favoring the upper income groups. The most important consequence of this system of taxation is to limit considerably the tax-raising ability of local government, so that public services in large American cities typically fluctuate between barely adequate and inadequate. Any change in the tax structure would probably provide the common rallying point to unite local business groups against such reformist policies.

The absence of rent control also has consequences for the city's tax structure. Property taxes on landlords are partially passed on to the tenant in the form of rent increases, just as any local tax on business tends to be passed on to the consumer in the form of higher prices; hence the absence of local rent control means that city renters are paying an indirect tax to the city with each rent check. Since upper income groups pay a relatively smaller share of their income in rent, it is likely that this form of indirect taxation is also regressive. From all of these considerations it can be concluded that the tax and bond systems favor the upper classes, that even if local businessmen never set foot in city hall it is still their kind of policy which the city is promoting, and that such a policy contributes to the problems of the low- and middle-income groups.

The facts of influence over elections, over the design of the government itself, and over the tax system, as well as the dependency of government on support from private leaders, offers a total pattern of influence at variance with the traditional view of business influence at the local level. Political scientists Edward Banfield and James Q. Wilson, in their book *City Politics,* lay down three requisites to a high degree of business influence in local politics:

> 1) Businessmen must have an interest in wielding local influence; 2) they must have a common set of goals, either because they agree or because they can be made to agree by some centralizing influence in the business community; and 3) they must control those resources valued by the politicians and thus control the politicians.[4]

For Oakland condition 3 is largely fulfilled: local businessmen offer vital support for local projects and bond issue campaigns in several forms: funds for local electoral races; donated time of local executives, a practice common for the Kaiser and other companies; and column space and endorsements in the local paper. All of these resources desired by politicians are held, in abundant degree, by the city's business community. Condition 1 is also fulfilled; the business community has an enormous interest in wielding influence in the city to get large shares of Federal monies, in starting up projects for transportation and redevelopment to maintain the city's economic viability and in keeping taxes and bonded indebtedness at the lowest possible levels. Indeed manifestation of interest in city politics by local businessmen is one of the most notable features of the city's politics.

Condition 2 is the hardest to achieve in any local community, yet we can find it occurring in Oakland at several points in the city's history. On many issues, such as the location of a bay bridge and the planning department decisions on traffic flows, uptown and downtown businesses are divided. But on other issues, and on the basics of city policies, they are united. The business community was completely united during the 1930s in opposing unionization of public and private employees and the growth of the CIO. It united vocally, publicly, and unequivocally to denounce the General Strike in 1947, and to press its viewpoint on the city government. It has offered less dramatic but generally broad-based support in the passage of major public welfare bonds of 1935 and the major post-1945 bond issues. It united, in OCCUR, to create the redevelopment program. Hence the active, direct involvement of the whole business community has been a prominent feature of business political activity in the city's recent history. Equally important is the current consensus of business along a range of issues that are part of the ruling consensus of city politics and which, as a result, make constant business involvement unnecessary: acceptance of trade unions, acceptance of Federal aid for cities, and acceptance of a policy by local police of surveillance and prosecution of Black Panthers and other radicals in the community. Here, if business *wanted* the city to change its policy and brought pressure to bear, it could effect a very substantial change. In short the unity of the business community on political issues is as well demonstrated by business *non*intervention as by active intervention.

THE SPECIALIZED INFLUENCE OF BUSINESS

Besides their leading influence over the political system, the city's business leaders have injected themselves into the political scene in particular areas of policy of importance to them and their firms. In the area of port management and operation, private businessmen are the primary source of policy making. In the area of housing policies, the above pages have shown that the city's real estate interests have become involved in city politics on many occasions and with an over-all record of success: in repealing rent control, writing the various building codes, emasculating a strong enforcement provision against slumlords, approving limited amounts of public housing, and opposing any city action against segregation in housing. In all of these activities the city's realtors have played an active role, either as an effective opposition, as in the case of antislumlord provision and the repeal of rent control, or in providing advice and consent. City elected officials have shown a willingness to listen to the real estate board, and when a contest is involved, not to listen to renters.

We find the same pattern of decisive involvement for economic reasons in the case of regional planning activity, rapid transit (BART), and redevelopment projects. All of these have been initiated or given necessary support so that business can maintain the functioning and profitability of its center city investments, and, as noted in Table 7-5, we find that business assumes a role not only in the creation of the programs, but in their direct administration to a much greater extent than any other private sector of society.

This leaves the areas of economic dependency programs, areas in which business can derive substantial economic benefit, depending on how the programs are designed. Dependency programs are not primarily intended to improve the profit-making ability of local firms, but are clearly related to the level of articulated social unrest and the possibility of violent destruction of local business properties. Hence this area, too, meets Banfield's first prerequisite for a high degree of potential business influence, and as the possibilities of urban rioting continue the motivation for business involvement in economic dependency programs will continue.

The jobs, economic development, and poverty programs demonstrate that, not in just a few cases, but in almost all cases in which a significant amount of public energy and resources were to be spent on a program, certain corporations were involved either in a role of major support or in initiating or administering any program. In the Interagency Project which preceded the poverty program the *Tribune* and the chamber of commerce provided money and manpower, as well as official sanction to the program. In the poverty program itself, businessmen initially controlled the OEDC, the top policy board of the program, while the local activist corporations continue to supply support to the program today. The greatest job program undertaken on local initiative, the Adult Minority Employment Project, was initiated by the Kaiser company and governmental officials, while the Skill Center received support of business representatives on the county MDTA council. Business has acted as administrator, or shared administrative authority with other governmental authorities, in the majority of major job training programs, including the Adult Minority Employment Project, JOBS, and the now-defunct Job Corps center for the Western states. None of these programs have threatened business priorities or forced business to change its hiring practices; on the contrary several of them, by subsidizing employers for on-the-job training, have resulted in substantial additional revenue to local employers. And no new jobs in the government sector, which would make government a competitive employer, have been established, a non-event of substantial importance to the city's growing number of unemployed. And it bears repeating that substantial monies have been used since 1945 for industrial development and not for job creation or maximization, an ordering of priorities in which the unemployed had no voice.

If there is a substantial direct influence by business in job and poverty programs and an adherence by the public sphere to private corporate priorities, then what of welfare? Can it be said that there is corporate involvement, or even decisive influence, in matters relating to welfare? The answer here on the basis of the Oakland experience is clearly yes. The welfare system must be understood as a part of the larger political regime, a necessary part of the urban system which draws the grudging consent of local elites. The alternative to welfare, with its sub-subsistence allotments for the poor, is starvation or sterilization, and neither the city's businessmen nor politicians are ready for that. Thus the willingness of local elites to tolerate welfare is a basic reason for the program's survival.

The more direct influence of business and the *Tribune,* like that of county labor groups and Democrats, is exercised over welfare policy through the county board of supervisors. The below-subsistence level of welfare allotments receive heavy support at the polls from working and middle-class voters who view the welfare caste as lazy dregs responsible for their own poverty, an attitude which the news columns of the local paper do not dispel. Given its power over elections to the county board, the *Tribune* can be said to be, in large measure, an arbiter of welfare levels in the county.

Despite the above kinds and instances of influence it might still be argued that business does not *rule,* for two reasons. First, this volume has shown that big or medium business is not the only important source of influence in local politics, that labor and blacks have, at various times, played important power roles. Secondly, and derived from this, is the fact that business does not always win exactly what it wants. The election of four labor representatives to the city council in 1947 and the failure of the city council to establish a department of building and safety as demanded by OCCUR in 1957 are notable cases of business defeats. In the case of the urban renewal and poverty programs, certain important decisions—stopping the farming out of welfare recipients to strawberry growers, the growth of a county welfare workers union, the maintenance of a strong black power faction on the poverty program's governing board, and the strong representation of the Black Caucus on the Model Cities Policy Committee, have not favored business interests and were won only by militant fights against the bureaucracy waged by poor and neighborhood groups and welfare workers.

The test of the existence of a ruling or predominant group in urban politics is not, however, whether the group in question *always* wins exactly what it wants. No ruling group in history fulfills such a requirement. The appropriate test is whether on a majority or disproportionately large number of cases in which it takes an interest, one social group's wishes become official policy, while the wishes of other groups are not articulated, are ignored, or are successfully combatted. Under this test the city's large and medium businesses qualify as the major political force in the city's politics. While other sectors were important in relating to sources of systemic and particularistic influence, no other sector in society provided nearly as much influence, in a variety of forms, as the city's business leaders. And equally important we can say that the structure and tax systems of local government impose such restraints on the autonomy of public administration and legislation that no adequate program of eliminating ghettos, poverty, and underemployment is possible within the present framework of local finance.

WHO BENEFITS? THE OTHER HALF OF URBAN POLITICS

This essay has tried to introduce the question of benefits, the differential impact of policy, as a basic question in the methodology of community research. It has dealt with this question in several ways. First, the chapters dealing with policy areas have presented extensive evidence that the government's programs are not meeting the needs of the city for jobs and housing, and that in many cases government activity is aggravating the problem. Thus the failure of the business system to allocate resources in a certain way is recapitulated by the same failure on the part of government—due in large part, as these chapters indicate, to the power of industry over public policy. Secondly these chapters show that these programs which the government has undertaken have been undertaken in such a way as to guarantee benefits for the affected businessmen and, often but not always, to minimize possible benefits for the laboring poor. Indeed, it is accurate to say that the public policy process generally has tended to *increase* the incomes of the rich and the nonincomes of the poor, quite the opposite of any redistribution effect.

The present distribution of benefits was not required by the logic of the Oakland situation. Programs for renewal or public housing represent social needs, and the question of whether these needs are filled, and who benefits from programs attempting to fill them is a matter of conscious choice, of political policy. And it was often policy in Oakland, until the Black Caucus and even after, to minimize benefits for the poor. In urban renewal, a $2 million subsidy was deliberately given to local business, while the poor were driven out of the demolition area; in private housing, the city granted permits to build almost all the new, privately constructed postwar units in the affluent areas and almost none in the poor nonwhite areas. In public housing, the city has built very few units, although there was Federal money in the form of a program reservation available for additional public housing for the ghetto poor. Federal job programs, based on the idea of retraining or on-the-job training without the creation of new jobs, resulted in guaranteed profits to corporate employers who took trainees, but have not increased the job supply. Meanwhile BART and other construction projects have removed additional thousands of dwellings from the city's housing stock. The city's code enforcement program has barely held the line on deterioration, while it has forced owners too poor to meet requirements to close their buildings. In all of these areas, the *ways* in which public programs were administered often contained within them a bias against the poor and nonwhite, the lesser and nonpropertied groups of the city.

Finally, the city, by staying out of the area of business operation or regulation, allows the private owners to control the assets of the city, to manipulate those assets in accordance with noncommunity, profit-oriented values, and hence to control the basic allocation of resources in the city. By preserving that set of practices and economic power the local government preserves the basic interests of the economic dominants and guarantees the continued existence of many of the city's economic problems. It is important to note that this primary interest of city businessmen is protected, while the primary interest of the poor—to get out of poverty—is not.

Thus, across the widest range of public policies and in the protection of their basic interest, the city's medium and large businessmen have reaped the major and continuing benefits of local policy, while the nonrich have reaped a harvest of more crowded housing, forced removal, relatively higher taxes, and minimum public services. Such organizations as unions and neighborhood groups have influenced the policy process to some extent as pressure groups, but so far have been unable to influence either the election or appointment of major city or county officials, or to bring about the redirection of public monies toward a broad-based effort to solve the problems of the poor or working classes. To call this a government of all the people would be a fiction. It would be more descriptive to speak of the city's political system as operating in the context of an economic system which has preponderant influence over public policies and which allows scope only to those public solutions which do not encroach on the interests of the private economy. In this situation, heavy or increased taxation of business or municipal ownership of utilities or other enterprises finds no advocates among urban politicians.

This system of power and policy formation has led to protest, rebellion, and militant organization by those whose interests have not been elevated to the level of policy—unorganized labor as long as 30 years ago and nonwhites today. This study of power in an urban context has shown the extent to which a very small set of persons and interests can find real expression in the current political organs of a city. Hopefully it has not only provided an insight into the organization of urban power, of who rules and for whom, but also an understanding of the need for informed opposition to the present system of urban political economy.

NOTES

1. James Weinstein, *The Decline of Socialism in America,* New York: Knopf, 1969, p. 103.
2. A useful discussion of patterns of labor involvement in California politics is in J. David Greenstone, *Labor in American Politics,* New York: Random House, 1969, chap. 5 and pp. 296-304.
3. For an excellent study of the extent to which local governments depend on business for support of school and other bond issues, see Ralph Kimbrough, *Political Power and Educational Decision Making,* Chicago: Rand McNally, 1964.
4. Edward Banfield and James Q. Wilson, *City Politics,* New York: Random House, 1966, p. 276.

Index